Egyptian Glyphary

A Sign List Based Hieroglyphic Dictionary of Middle Egyptian

compiled by

Bill Petty, PhD

D1667951

Museum Tours Press
Littleton, Colorado

Published by

Museum Tours Press
A division of
Museum Tours, Inc.
7110 Old farm Road
Littleton, CO 80128

www.museum-tours.com

ISBN - 978-1-48100-745-0

Cover Image: Inscription on the base of Hatshepsut's Obelisk in Karnak. Photo by Bill Petty

Version

14-1

Introduction

This paperback Glyphary™, or Sign List based Hieroglyphic Dictionary, is a companion to the **Hieroglyphic Sign List** and the **Hieroglyphic Dictionary**. It was developed to provide the interested student, amateur or profession with a handy reference to the Egyptian language. It is not organized alphabetically, like a regular dictionary. Rather it has been organized according to the hieroglyphic signs. In order to maintain ease of use, the order and the numbering generally follow the sign list in Gardiner's Egyptian Grammar. Variations of a sign are indicated by adding a letter to the Gardiner number. Signs that are not listed by Gardiner are given numbers beginning with 80.

To look up a word one need only find a prominent sign in the word, look it up, then proceed to examine the subsequent, alphabetical listings for the desired word. In order to maintain a reasonable ease of use, indexing is based on a signs "recognition factor". On a scale of 1 to 5, a recognition factor of 1 means that the sign is practically useless for indexing a word. This is normally because the sign is so common in so many words that using it for look-up would be virtually useless. On the other hand, a recognition factor of 5 indicates that that the sign can be used to find the definition of a word with little or no ambiguity.

The following signs have a recognition factor of **1**, that is, they are so common that they are not used in indexing words except where absolutely necessary:

The alphabetical (uniliteral) signs have a recognition factor of **2** and are not used in indexing words, except in those cases where they are at the beginning of a word and the word contains no sign with a higher recognition factor (**3**, **4** or **5**)

The following signs (generally determinatives and biliterals) have a recognition factor of **3** and are used for indexing only in those cases where the word contains no sign with a recognition factor of **4** or **5**. This group also contains signs that are easily confused with other signs and signs that are often used interchangeably with another sign (such as the strong arm and the strong man).

Signs with recognition factor of **4** are similar to those with a factor of **3**, except that they are not as common. They are generally used for indexing when the word does not contain any sign with a factor of **5**.

The vast majority of signs (about 700) have a recognition factor of **5**. They are used for indexing in all word in which they appear and finding a word containing the sign is rather straightforward because there are not too many words to search through.

The recognition factor of each sign is listed as an aid in determining if you have selected a good sign for your search.

Organization

Signs are listed, generally, in the order and numbering followed in Gardiner's Egyptian Grammar. The Gardiner Sign Number is followed by the sign itself, its recognition factor in parenthesis, and its associated sound and general meaning (if a determinative). Following the sign is a list of words, in generally alphabetical order, that contain that particular sign. In the case of the alphabetical characters, a word is listed only if the sign is the first letter of the word (excluding prefixes).

Each word is represented by it spelling in Hieroglyphs (with several variations listed where appropriate).

This is followed by the words transliteration in ***bold italics***.

The definition of the word follows in regular type.

Explanatory notes are included in parentheses.

Brackets, [ ] , are used to indicate additional characters commonly used with the current word, with corresponding transliteration and definition also in [ ] .

For more detailed information on the individual signs, one should consult the "Hieroglyphic Sign List" by the same author.

Spelling: The Egyptians rarely let themselves be confined to only one way to spell a word. As a result there are often several different variations in the spelling of various words. It is also common to omit certain letters, typically ***i*** and ***y***. In our spelling we have generally included the simplest version and some variations, where appropriate. We have also included letters in the transliteration (usually ***i*** and ***y***), even when these letters have been omitted from the actual hieroglyphic spelling. When the hieroglyphic spelling of a word does not match the actual transliteration, the Hieroglyphic spelling takes precedence in the listing. Thus  which is actually transliterated as ***ḫft*** is listed under ***ḫtf***. In those rare cases where an obscure determinative is used it will sometimes be replaced with a similar sign or by a simple crosshatch pattern, .

Abbreviations: Abbreviations and informational comments are printed in regular type and enclosed in parentheses. Abbreviations used:

fem - feminine	suf - suffix
masc - masculine	pre - prefix
LE - Lower Egypt	O - Old Egyptian
UE - Upper Egypt	L - Late Egyptian
id - idiomatic expression	lit - literally

We always strive to improve our products. If you have any comments, suggestions or corrections, please email them to mt@museum-tours.com, with the subject line “Egyptian Glyphary”.

Acknowledgements

The origins of the modern Hieroglyphic Sign List are somewhat obscure. In his 1910 book, *Egyptian Language*, E. A. Wallis Budge credited Adolph Holzhausen with the classifications and numbering of the signs known at that time. The numbering has totally changed over the years, but the classifications are still largely used today.

In his 1915 book, *Egyptian Hieroglyphic Grammar*, Gunther Roeder used the same classifications and numbering that Budge used in 1910, but he credited Karl Richard Lepsius for their origin.

Regardless of who created the classification and numbering, there can be no doubt that Alan Gardiner in his 1926 classic, *Egyptian Grammar*, set the standard that has been used, with minor modification, and considerable addition, ever since.

The organization of this book is based on Gardiner's standard Sign List, except that added signs are indicated with lowercase letters following the number, rather than the asterisk used by Gardiner (e.g. Gardiner's **D46*** is **D46a**). A few additions have also been made to Gardiner's list.

In addition to the author's own observations, much is owed to the following for the contents of this work: E. Wallis Budge, Mark Collier, Raymond Faulkner, Alan Gardiner, Bill Manley, Kurt Sethe, Karl-Theodor Zauzich.

The hieroglyphic fonts were based on InScribe, a product of Saqqara Technology.

My heartfelt thanks to my wife Nancy for putting up with me during compilation of this book.

Table of Contents

Page		
3		Introduction
5		Organization
7		Acknowledgements
9		Phonetic Alphabet
10	A	Man
30	B	Woman
32	C	Anthropomorphic Gods
34	D	Parts of the Human Body
67	E	Mammals
76	F	Parts of Mammals
96	G	Birds
116	H	Parts of Birds
118	I	Amphibians, Reptiles, etc
123	K	Fish & Parts of Fish
126	L	Invertebrates & Lesser Animals
128	M	Trees & Plants
148	N	Sky, Earth, Water
173	O	Buildings
188	P	Ships & Parts of Ships
193	Q	Furniture
197	R	Temple Accoutrements
202	S	Crowns, Dress, Staves
214	T	Warfare & Hunting
226	U	Agriculture & Crafts
242	V	Rope, Fiber, Baskets, Bags, etc
256	W	Vessels of Stone & Earthenware
267	X	Loaves & Cakes
271	Y	Writing, Games, Instruments
274	Z	Strokes, Signs, Figures
280	Aa	Unclassified
289		Index to Sign List
294		Index by Shape

The Phonetic Alphabet

Phonetic Character		**English Pronunciation**
ꜣ	>	“a” as in the cockney ‘arp (for harp)
i	>	“i” as in ink
y	>	“y” as in any
ꜥ	>	“a” as in far
w	>	“w” as in wet (beginning of word)
		“u” as in duty (within a word)
b	>	“b” as in bed
p	>	“p” as in pet
f	>	“f” as in fed
m	>	“m” as in met
n	>	“n” as in net
r	>	“r” as in red
h	>	“h” as in hen
ḥ	>	“h”, but from the throat
ḫ	>	“kh”, like “ch” in Scottish “loch”
ẖ	>	“k”, like “ch” in German “ich”
s	>	“s” as in set
š	>	“sh” as in shed
ḳ	>	“q”, but without the u
k	>	“k” as in keg
g	>	“g” as in get
t	>	“t” as in ten
ṯ	>	“ch” as in chess (sometimes written as “tch” or “tj”
d	>	“d” as in den
ḏ	>	“j” as in jet (sometimes written as “dj”)

A - Man

1  (3) *man, relationships, occupations*

 ***i*** I, me, my

 ***i(w)ˁyt*** garrison, soldiery, troops

 ***ink*** I, me, my

 ***irr*** doer

 ***it*** father

 ***wi*** I, me, my

 ***wr*** great one, chief, prince

 ***bṯnw, btnw*** defiant man, rebel

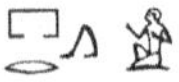 ***pry*** hero, champion

 ***mwnf*** garrison

 ***nb*** lord, master, owner (of) (used before modified word)

 ***rmṯ*** man, men, people, mankind

 ***rḫ*** wise man

 ***rḥw*** men, fellows

 ***ḥwrw*** wretch

 ***ḥkr*** hungry man

 ***ẖnms*** friend

 ***r i*** (gives emphasis to "I")

 ***s(i)*** man, someone, anyone, person

 ***sꜣ*** son

 ***smr*** courtier, friend

 ***smdt*** subjects, subordinates, staff

 ***snhy*** to record, muster (troops)

 ***kw(i)*** other, another

 ***kwi*** I, me, my

 ***grw*** silent one

 ***tꜣy i*** my

A - Man (cont)

ỉt father

thr a Syrian warrior

tšw deserter

1a (3) *people and their occupations*

ꜣbt family, relatives

ꜥꜣmw Asiatics

pꜥt patricians, mankind

mhwt family, household

mšꜥ army

hnw neighbors, associates, family

rmṯ man, men, mankind, people

sꜣḥw neighbors, dependents

smdt subjects, subordinates, staff

ḏt serfs

2 (3) *eat, drink, speak, think, feel*

ꜣbꜣb be delighted

ꜣbỉ to desire

ỉ "O"

ỉ to say

ỉn says

ỉꜣš call

ỉꜣꜥnw lamentation, sorrow, woe

ỉb suppose, imagine

ỉmỉ to mourn

ỉnyt refrain (of song)

ỉnn we

ꜥbꜥ boast, exaggerate

A - Man (cont)

ꜥm to swallow, know

ꜥnꜥn to complain, complaint

ꜥš call

ꜥš-ḥꜣt pilot

wꜥꜣ speak abuse, curse

wfꜣ talk, talk about, discuss

wnm eat

wšꜥ bite, chew

wšb answer

wšbw comforter

bỉt character, qualities

prw motion, procession, result

mskỉ rumor

msḏỉ hate

nỉs invoke, summon, recite

nỉsw one summoned

nhp to care (for)

nhm jubilate

nḥỉ pray (for)

nḥṯ prayer

nẖwt complaint, mourning

nkꜣ [m] reflect [upon], think [about]

nkꜣt plot

nḏb sip

nḏt subjects, serfs

rn name

hy Hail!, shout

hmhmt roaring, war cry, squawking

A - Man (cont)

ḥkn exult, be joyful, acclaim

ḥknw exultation, praise, thanksgiving

ḥḳr be hungry, hunger

ḥḳr hungry man

sbi drink

snḥy to record, muster (troops)

sr official, noble

srḫ complain, accuse

sḥwr vilify

sgr quiet

sḏdw stories

sḏdt description

šbi to change, alter, mix, mingle, confuse

kꜣ soul, personality, mood, attribute, fortune, will (of king)

kꜣ so, then

kꜣi think about, plan, so, then

kꜣt thought, plan, device, plot

ki [ḥr] cry out loud, complain [about]

kni be sullen

gr be silent, quiet, still, silence, cease, desist

grw silent one

ṯnf enjoyment

ṯḥw rejoice, exultation, joy

dm pronounce, proclaim (a name), be renowned

ḏws malign

ḏꜣis to contend, dispute, argue, oppose

ḏꜣisw disputant

ḏꜣrw need, requirement

A - Man (cont)

3 (5) *sit, dwell, besiege*

ꜥḥꜥ ḥmsi pass one's life

ḥmsi sit, sit down, dwell, besiege

ḥmsi ḥr besiege

ḥmst council (of the king and courtiers)

ḥmsw sloth

4 (5) *supplicate, adore, hide*

imn, imnw, imnt hide, secret, conceal

ḥtpyw non-combatants

sdẖ hide

sdgꜣ [r] hide or conceal [from]

sdgw hidden things

dwꜣ adore

dgi hide

5 (5) *hide*

imn hide, secret, conceal

kꜣp to cover, hide

6 (5) *purify*

wꜥb pure, clean

s(ꜣ)ṯ libation stone

7 (5) *weary, weak, soft, faint, tire* (see also **A3**)

wrd, wrḏ tire, be weary

bꜣgi be remiss, slack, weary

bꜣgyw the dead

bdš faint, weak, exhausted, helpless

bdšt weakness

nḏw miller

A - Man (cont)

 ***ḥmsi*** sit, sit down, dwell, besiege

 ***s'3y*** tremble

 ***srf*** rest, repose

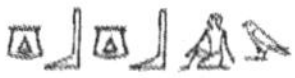 ***gbgb*** be lame, fell (an enemy)

,  ***gnn*** be soft, weak

 ***gtḥ*** be tired

 ***sgnn*** soften, weaken

 ***dgi*** hide

8  (5) *jubilation, praise*

 ***hnw*** jubilation, praise

 ***hnw*** neighbors, associates, family

9  (5) *work, load carry*

 [], ,  ***3tp [m], 3tp*** to load [with]

 ***3tpw*** load

,  ***f3i*** carry, lift, weigh

 ***f3i3w*** to sail

, ,  ***k3t*** work, construction

10  (5) *sailor, traveler*

,  ***sḳd*** sailor, traveler

11  (5) *friend*

,  ***ḫnms*** friend, associate with

12  (5) *army, soldier*

 ***pḫrt*** frontier guard

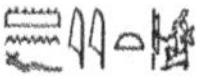, ,  ***mnfyt, mnf3t*** soldiers, assault troops

, ,  ***mš'*** army

,  ***mš'*** expedition

A - Man (cont)

13 (5) *enemy, rebel*

itnw opponent

ꜥnḫ captive

mryn Syrian warrior

nḥsy Nubian

rst sacrificial victims, foreign hordes

ḥꜣḳw captives

ḫꜣrw one from Khor

ḫft(y), ḫtf enemy

ḫꜣkw-ib disaffected, rebel

sbi rebel

sḳr captive

sḳr-ꜥnḫ captive

ḳꜣt foes

ḳdw enemies from Kode

tkkw attackers

13a (5) (as above)

14 (5) *die, death, enemy*

ꜣꜣtꜣ Nubian chieftain (?) or his name (?)

ꜣw deceased (lit - extended)

ꜥbw victims

bšttyw rebels

bṯnw, btnw defiant man, rebel

m(w)t die, death

mni death, die

mnṯ(y)w Beduins of Asia

mgꜣ skirmisher

A - Man (cont)

mt die, death

rst sacrificial victims, foreign hordes

rḳ ib disaffected one, rebel

rḳw enemy

rtt conspiracy

ḫbyt carnage, slaughter, destruction

ḫpyt death

ḫfty enemy

ḫnrtt conspiracy

sbit rebels

sḏryt slaughter

šm(ꜣ)w wanderers, strangers, foreigners

šnṯy foe

14a (5) (as above)

15 (5) *fall, defeated, enemy, overthrow*

ḫꜣyt slaughter, massacre

ḫr fall, defeated

ḫr and, further

ḫrw (defeated) enemy

ḫrw low lying land

ẖtb overthrow, kill

sḫr overthrow, force into place

sḫrt overthrow, defeat

sṯsy be stretched out, prostrate

sḏr lie prostrate

sḏryt slaughter

gbgb be lame, fell (an enemy)

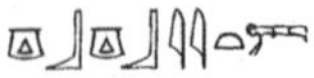 ***gbgbyt*** fall headlong, prostate

16  **(5)** *bow down*

 ***nyny*** to do homage, greeting

 ***ksi*** to bow down

17  **(5)** ***nni*** *young, child*

 ***iḥms*** occupant (in titles), attendant

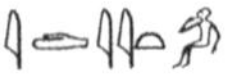 ***idyt*** girl, maid

 ***wḏḥ*** weaned princeling

 ***msꜣ*** young recruits

 ***msw*** children

 ***mswtt*** girl child

 ***mgꜣ*** young recruits

 ***nw*** be weak, limp

 ***nmḥ*** be poor, deprive (of)

 ***nmḥ(y)*** orphan, low class person

 ***nni-nsw*** Heracleopolis (UE)

 ***nḫn*** be young, child

 ***nḫnw*** youth

 ***rnp*** young man

 ***rnpi*** be young, vigorous

 ***rnpw*** youthful vigor

 ***ḥꜥꜣw*** children

 ***ḥwn*** youthful, youth, vigor, be young, refreshed, child, young man

 ***ḥwnt*** maiden

 ***ḥwrw*** wretch

 ***ẖrd*** child

A - Man (cont)

ẖrdw childhood

ẖrdt children

snẖn to nurse

sḏty child, foster child

šri lad, boy, child, younger son

ḏꜣmw young men, troops

17a

(5) (as **A17** or **A3**)

18

(5) *prince, child king*

inp(w) crown prince, royal child

wḏḥ weaned princeling

19

(5) ***ik*** *old, eldest, great, lean (on), support, chief, prince*

iꜣwi be old, attain old age

iꜣ(y)t old woman

iꜣw old man

iꜣwt old age

iky stone cutter, miner

wr great one, chief, prince

rhn lean

rhn ḥr lean upon, drive in, tread

ḥwi, ḥii strike, hit

smsw eldest

twꜣ to support, lean

tni old, decrepit

20

(5) (as above)

21

(5) *official, nobleman, magnate, statue, associate*

bwꜣw magnates

A - Man (cont)

ẖnms friend, associate with

ẖnt(y) statue

ḳnbt court of magistrates

smr friend, courtier

sr official, noble

srwt office, magistracy

srt office, magistracy

šnyt courtiers

22 (5) *statue, image*

ẖnt(y) statue, image

twt statue, image

23 (5) *sovereign*

ity sovereign

ityt queen regent

24 (3) *effort, force, strike, strength* (see also **D40**)

ꜣwi extend, stretch out

ꜣwy extend

ꜣwḥ do violence

ꜣmi [ḥr] mix, compound [with]

ꜣr [ḥr] restrain, hold back [from], drive away, oppress

ꜣwi extend, stretch out

iꜥi wash

iꜥi ib satisfy (one's) desire, appetite, wrath

ihm hold back, detain

ikn draw (water)

itn oppose, thwart

iṯꜣ thief

A - Man (cont)

ꜥwn defraud, rapacious, covetous, despoil

ꜥmꜥ smear [mud]

ꜥfty brewer

ꜥtḫ to strain (liquid)

wꜥf bend, curb

wn open

wn ḥr instructed, expert

bḥ forced labor

bšṯ be rebellious, rebellion

pis tread in (corn)

pnḳ bail out

ptpt trample down, crush

pds stamp flat

fꜣi carry, lift, weigh

fꜣi ṯꜣw sail (lit - carry the wind)

nbḏ destructive

nri be in terror

nḥm take away, rescue

nḫt strong, victory, victorious, strength

ḫꜣꜥb bad quality

ḥꜥḏꜣ plunder, plunderer

ḥwi, ḥii strike, beat, drive in, tread

ḥw-ny-r-ḥr combat

ḫꜣi examine

ḫnp rob, despoil, offer

ḫdb kill

sꜣb cross (water)

sbꜣ teach

A - Man (cont)

snẖt to strengthen

sẖs to run, hurry

ḳn brave man

ḳni be strong, prevail over, strong man, strong, dutiful, brave

titi crush, trample down

tpt-rd task

ḏꜣis argument, dispute

ḏꜣytyw opponents

25 (5) *strike*

ḥ(wi), ḥ(ii) strike, beat, drive in, tread (a road)

59 (5) *drive away, banish*

rḥwy two combatants

sḥri drive away, banish

titi crush, trample down

26 (5) *summon, call, servant*

i "O"

nis invoke, summon, recite, servant

sḏm ꜥš servant

dwi to call

27 (5) *in*

in by

28 (5) *high, joy, extol, rejoice, mourn, bald*

iꜣs bald

ihhy jubilation

wꜣš be exalted, be strong, be honored

hnw jubilation, praise

ḥꜣi mourn

A - Man (cont)

 ***ḥʿi*** rejoice, joyful

 ***ḥʿʿw*** rejoice

 ***ḥʿʿwt*** joy

 ***ḥʿwt*** joy

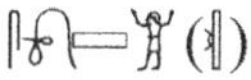 ***swꜣš*** extol

 ***sḳꜣ*** shrine base

 ***sḳꜣi*** raise, prolong, set right

 ***ḳꜣi*** be high, tall, loud, exalted

 ***ḳꜣyt*** high ground, arable land

 ***ḳꜣw*** height

 ***ḳꜣt*** height

29  **(5)** *upside down*

 ***sḫd*** upside down, head down

30  **(5)** *praise, supplicate, awe*

 ***iꜣw*** praise

 ***swꜣš*** extol

 ***šm(ꜣ)w*** wanderers, strangers, foreigners

 ***twꜣ*** claim

 ***twꜣ*** poor man, inferior

 ***twr [ḥr]*** show respect [for]

 ***tri*** show respect for

 ***tryt*** respect

 ***dwꜣ*** adore

31  **(5)** *turn away, avert one's face*

 ***ʿnw*** avert (one's face)

 ***ʿnn*** turn back

A - Man (cont)

32  (5) *dance, joy, jubilate*

 ***iꜣḳ*** to leap

 ***ibꜣ*** dance

 ***rwi*** dance

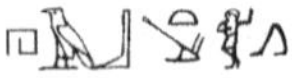 ***hꜣbt*** dance

 ***hy hnw*** jubilate

 ***ẖbi*** to dance

 ***ẖbt*** dance

33  (5) *wander(er), stranger, herder*

 ***mniw*** herdsman, assault troops

 ***rwi*** wander

 ***smntyw*** emissaries

 ***šm(ꜣ)w*** wanderers, strangers, foreigners

34  (5) *pound , tamp, build*

 ***ẖwsi*** pound , tamp, build, accomplish

35  (5) *build*

 ***ḳd*** build, fashion (pots), form

 ***sḳd*** cause to build

 ***ḳd*** builder

36  (5) *brewer*

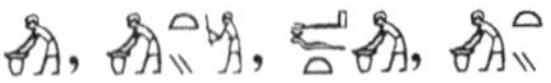 ***ꜥfty*** brewer

37  (5) (as above)

38  (5)

 ***ḳis*** city of Cusae (UE)

39  (5) (as above)

A - Man (cont)

40  **(3)** *a god, (sometimes the king)*

 ***ꜣkr*** (god) Aker

 ***i, wi, ink*** I, me (god or king)

 ***iꜥḥ*** moon

 ***ipt*** festival of the 12th month

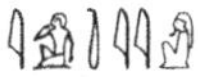 ***ity*** sovereign

 ***itm*** (god) Atum

 ***wp-wꜣwt*** (the wolf god) Wepwawet

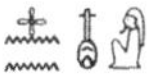 ***wn-nfr*** Osiris

 ***wsir*** (god) Osiris

 ***bsw*** secret image

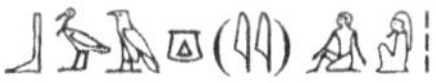 ***bꜣgyw*** the dead

 ***pꜣwty*** primeval god

 ***pwntyw*** the people of Punt

 ***ptḥ*** (god) Ptah

 ***mr-wr*** Menevis bull

 ***mḫnty*** ferry boat operator

 ***mstw*** offspring

 ***nsw*** King (of Upper Egypt)

 ***nṯr*** god, divine

 ***rꜥ*** (god) Ra

 ***rḥwy*** Ra & Thoth or Horus & Seth

 ***ḥpy*** (god) Hepy (son of Horis)

 ***ḥr*** (falcon god) Horus

 ***ḫm*** sacred image

 ***ḫmnyw*** the 8 deities of Hermopolis

 ***sꜣḥ*** (constellation) Orion

A - Man (cont)

s3ty-bity the royal twins, Shu & Tefnet

s3ty-gb "son of **Geb**"

sšmw divine shape, form, statue

ḳbḥ-snw-f a son of Horus

gb (earth god) **Geb**

gnbtw foreigners from Punt

gmḥsw hawk

dw3-mut a son of Horus

ddwn a Nubian god

ḏḥwty (god) Thoth

41 (5) *king*

i, wi, ink I, me (king)

inp(w) crown prince, royal child

nsyw kings

nsw king

ḥm majesty

42 (5) (as above)

43 (5) *king of Upper Egypt, king*

wsir Osiris

nsyw kings

nsw, ni-swt king of Upper Egypt, king

44 (5) (as above)

45 (5) *king of Lower Egypt, king*

bity king of Lower Egypt

46 (5) (as above)

A - Man (cont)

47 (5) *guard, protect*

ỉry relating to, belonging to

m(ỉ)nỉw herdsman

sꜣỉ linger, lag

sꜣw guard, protect, ward off, restrain, beware lest

sꜣw guardian, warden

sꜣwt stand guard against, watch

sꜣwty guardian

48 (5) *relating to, belonging to*

ỉry relating to, belonging to

ỉrt duty, use, purpose

ỉryw (boat's) crew

ỉry nfr ḫꜣt keeper of the diadem

ỉry sšm functionary

ỉry ḫt administrator

ỉry rdwy attendant

ỉry ꜥꜣ door keeper

ỉrt duty

49 (5) *foreigner*

ꜣḫty of a remote people

ỉwntyw styw Nubian bowmen

ꜥꜣmw Asiatics

ḫbstyw bearded ones of Punt

50 (5) *noble or revered* (person), *splendid* (thing)

ỉ, wỉ, ỉnk I, me

ỉmyw-ḥꜣt those of former times

 ***mity*** likeness

 ***sꜥḥ*** deceased noble

 ***smr(w)*** courtiers

 ***snḏm*** sit

 ***šps*** noble (act)

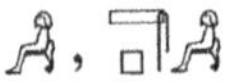 ***šps*** noble, revered (person), splendid (thing)

 ***špsi*** be noble, rich

 ***špss*** noble, august, esteemed

 ***špssw*** riches, wealth

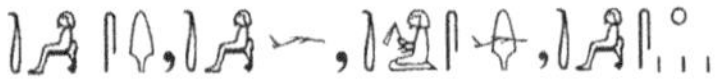 ***ti šps*** a tree, a spice

 ***tp-ꜥw(y)*** who are in front, before, ancestors, former

 ***ḏrtyw*** ancestors

51  (5) (as above)

52  (5) (as above)

53  (5) *form, mummy, statue, likeness, shape*

 ***irw*** form, nature

 ***wi*** mummy, mummy wrap

 ***rpyt*** statue of female

 ***mstw*** offspring

 ***ḫprw*** form, shape, upbringing, stages of growth

 ***ḫnty*** statue

 ***sꜥḥ*** mummy

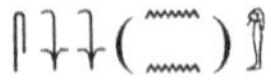 ***snn*** image, portrait

 ***stwt*** resemble, even out, praise

 ***šwbty*** ushabti figure

 ***šsp*** image

 ***ḳi*** form, image

A - Man (cont)

,  ***twt*** statue, image

 () ,  ***twt*** pleasing, fair, fitting, like

54  **(5)** *dead*

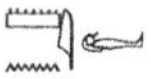 ***mni*** death, die

 ***nb ꜥnḫ*** sarcophagus

55  **(5)** *lie, death, sleep*

 ***ẖꜣt*** corpse

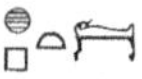 ***ḫpt*** decease, die, death

 ***ḳbḥ*** death

 ***ḳns*** bury

 ,  ***sḏr*** lie, spend the night, sleeping

59  **(5)** *drive away, banish*

 ***sḥr*** drive away, banish

81  (same as **A23,** ) (O)

82  (same as **A24,** ) (O)

B - Woman

1 **(5)** *woman, female, their occupations, relationships or names*

ꜣst (goddess) Isis

i I, me, my (fem)

iri ḥmt take a wife

bꜣstt (cat goddess) Bastet

mwt mother

mnt so and so, someone, such a one

mswt young children or animals

nt (goddess) **Neith**

nṯrt goddess

nḏtyw maid-servants

rmṯ man, men, mankind, people

rpyt statue of female

ḥmt wife, woman

ḥmt female slave

ḥnwt mistress

ḫꜣrt, ẖꜣrt widow

ḫbwt (female) dancers

ẖnm(t) nurse

ẖkrt concubine, hairdresser

sꜣt daughter

srḳt (goddess) Serket

snt sister

sẖt the marsh goddess

st woman

šmꜥyt chantress

tfnt (goddess) Tefenet

B - Woman (cont)

2 (5) *pregnant, conceive*

iwr conceive, become pregnant

bk3 be pregnant

3 (5) *give birth*

msi give birth, form, fashion

4 (5) (as above)

5 (5) *nurse, foster mother*

mnʿ to nurse, suckle

mnʿt nurse, foster mother

6 (5) *nurse, rear(a child)*

rnn nurse, rear (a child)

7 (5) *(name of) queen*

C - Anthropomorphic Gods

1 ,  ***rʿ*** Ra

2  (as above)

3 ,  ***ḏḥwty*** Thoth

,  ***iʿḥ*** moon

4 ,  ***ẖnmw*** Khnum

5  (as above)

6 ,  ***inpw*** Anubis

 ***wp-wꜣwt*** Wepwawet

7  ***stẖ, stš*** Seth

 ***nḳm*** be in pain, sorrow, suffer

 ***ẖꜣyt*** illness

8 ,  ***mnw*** Min

9 ,  ***ḥt ḥr*** Hathor

10 ,  ***mꜣʿt*** Maat

10a  (as above)

10b  (as above)

10c  (as above)

11  ***ḥḥ*** million, many, (the god) Heh

12  ***imn*** Amun

12a  (as above)

12b  (as above)

17  ***mnṯw*** Montu

C - Anthropomorphic Gods (Cont)

18 *tꜣ ṯnn* Tachenen (Tjanen)

18a (as above)

18b (as above)

19 *ptḥ* Ptah

19a (as above)

20 (as above)

81 (*god with double crown*) *a god*

82 ***i͗mn rꜥ*** Amun Ra

83 ***wsi͗r*** Osiris

85 ***ḥꜥpy*** Hapi

86 ***sḫmt*** Sekhmet

87 ***ḥr*** Horus

D - Parts of the Human Body

1 (5) ***tp*** *head ,chief, promote, behind, fetter, neglect, beginning, on*

pr r ḥꜣ go forth abroad

mkḥꜣ to neglect

ḥꜣ back of head, behind, around

ḥꜣ outside

gwꜣ tighten, besiege, be choked

gwꜣwꜣ fetter, bind fast, throttle, choke

gwꜣt chest

tp head, chief, tip, beginning (of time), upon

tp (number of) persons

tp-iꜣt due time (to act)

tpy chief, principal, first, who or which is upon

tpyw-ꜥ ancestors

tpyw-tꜣ the living

tp-ꜥ before, (into) the presence of

, , ***tp-ꜥw(y)*** who are in front, previous, ancestors

tp-wꜣt journey, beginning (of reign)

tp-m in the direction of, in front of

tp mꜣꜥ accompanying, escorting

tp-n-sšmt specification

, ***tp-rnpt*** feast of the first of the year

, ***tp(y)-r*** utterance

tp-rꜥ-mḏ 10 day week

tp-rd instructions, rules, principles

tp(y)-tꜣ survivor

tpt-rd task

tp-ḥwt roof

, ***tp-ḥsb*** reckoning, norm, standard, rectitude

D - Parts of the Human Body (cont)

tpt uraeus

tpt fine oil

tpt-ꜥ former state

tpt-r utterance

tpt-rd task

tpt--ḥr(y) master

tp-tr festival of the beginning of the season

dhn promote (to)

dhnt forehead

dhn tꜣ touch the forehead to the ground

ḏꜣḏꜣ head (of a group)

2 (5) *ḥr*

ꜣw ḥr farsighted

ꜥm ib ḥr be thoughtless, neglectful

wn ḥr instructed, expert

biꜣi, by [n] [ḥr] to wonder [at]

bs, ibs [ḥr] enter [into],

mr ḥr ib n be displeasing to

m ḥr f in his sight

nḥr resemble

r-ḥry master, chief

rdi m ib determine

rdi m ḥr n charge, command (person)

rdi r tꜣ to land, throw down, neglect

rdi ḥr gs partial, bias, dispose of, kill

rdit n r ḥr s "without neglecting my orders"

ḥw-ny-r-ḥr combat

D - Parts of the Human Body (cont)

ḥms(i) ḥr besiege

ḥr face, sight

ḥr upon, in, at, from, through, because, concerning, and, having on it, against

ḥr [r] be far, distant [from]

ḥr rope

ḥr (falcon god) Horus

ḥr prepare, terror, dread,

ḥry captain, chief, who is over, upper

[m] ḥr(y)-ib [in] the midst of

ḥr(y)-ib(y) who dwells in (said of deities)

ḥryw-rnpt epagomenal days

ḥryw-šꜥy Bedouin

ḥry-sꜣ a breed of cattle

ḥry-ẖt-f offering loaf

ḥryt dread

ḥry-tꜣ survivor

ḥry-tp chief, chieftain, who is upon, who is over

ḥr -ꜥ arrears, remainder

ḥr ꜥ, ḥr ꜥwy immediately

ḥrw upper part, top

ḥrw-r apart from, besides

ḥrf kind of bread

ḥr m why?

ḥr nb everyone

ḥr ntt because

ḥr-r be far from, besides

ḥrrt flower

D - Parts of the Human Body (cont)

ḥrst carnelian

ḥrt heaven, sky

ḥrt road

ḥrt hill-side tomb

ḥrt tomb

ḥrt-ib central hall (of a temple)

ḥrty travel (by land)

ḥrt-š garden

ḥrtt piece of lapis

ẖft-ḥr in the presence of, in front of

sꜣwy ḥr keep an eye on

sḥr [ ] fly, [ ] drive away, banish

sḥr fly aloft

sḥri drive away, banish

st-ḥr supervision

sḏꜣy ḥr divert oneself, amuse oneself

gs-ḥry top, uppermost

tpt--ḥr(y) master

dḥr bitter, sour

dḥr(i) skin, hide, leather

dḥrt bitterness, sickness

3 **(5)** *mourn, bald, empty, forlorn, hair, skin, defective*

iwn complexion, nature, color

inm skin

iꜣkb mourn

wpt top knot

wnwn sway, travel about

D - Parts of the Human Body (cont)

wš fall out, be bald, free, unoccupied

bbwt wig

fꜣk, fk be bald, bare

nšy dress (hair)

nšt hair-dresser

ḥnskt lock of hair

ḫꜣrt, ẖꜣrt widow

ḫbstyw bearded ones of Punt

sꜣmt mourning

smꜣ scalp, locks of hair

skm grey haired

šny hair

šnw hair

gm wš found defective, destroyed

gmḥt braided hair

gnbtw foreigners from Punt

ṯḥṯḥ disorder

4 (5) ***ir*** *see, blind, weep, wake, actions of the eye*

iꜣrrt vine

iri do, make, act, acquire, writing, achieving

ir-m amounting to

ir(i) m act for (someone)

ir-n, irt-n engendered by, amounting to

ir(i)-n act on behalf of, help

ir(i)-r act against, oppose

iri ḥmt take a wife

iri ḫt rituals (lit. "doing things")

iryt being done (or made), happened

D - Parts of the Human Body (cont)

irw form, shape, nature

irwy eyes

irr doer

irt eye

irtyw mourning

irtt milk

ꜥn a pleasant man

wnwt(y) hour watcher, astrologer

, *wsir* Osiris

, , , *mꜣꜣ* to see

mꜣꜣw sight

, *mꜣi* lion

mꜣw lions

mꜣw inspection

mꜣw aspect, appearance

mꜣr wretched

m-ir do not

nw see, look

( ) *nw* hunter

rmi to weep

rs be wakeful

smꜣwy renew, renovate

( ) *smꜣr* afflict, harm

, *sti* stare at

sdm eye paint

šp be blind

, ( ) *dgi* to look

D - Parts of the Human Body (cont)

5 (5) *action or conditions of the eye* (see also **D4**)

ꜥꜥw to sleep

ỉꜣrrt grapes

ptr behold, see

nhs wake up

( ) , ***rs*** be wakeful, be vigilant

rsw sentry, vigilance

sꜣwy ḥr keep an eye on

srs awaken, assume command

sgmḥ cause to see, glimpse

šp be blind

gmḥ look at

, , [ ] ***ggwy, ggwt [ḥr]*** dazzled, amazement, stare [at]

( ) ***di-rs-tp*** foreman

dgi to look

6 (5) (also as above) (see also **D4**))

ꜣḫt god's eye, eye of Ra

wbꜣ open courtyard

[ ] ***ggwy, ggwt [ḥr]*** dazzled, amazement, stare [at]

7 (5) ***ꜥn*** *adorn, beautiful, pleasant* (see also **D4**)

ꜥn beautiful, pleasing, kind

msḏmt eye paint

, ***ptr*** behold, see

8 (5) (see also **D7**)

ꜥn beautiful, pleasing kind

ꜥ(i)nw the Turah limestone quarry

D - Parts of the Human Body (cont)

9  **(5)** *weep*

,  ***rm(i)*** weep, beweep

 ***rmw*** weeping

 ***rmwt*** tears

10  **(5)**

,  ***wḏꜣt*** eye of Horus

11  **(5)** 1/2 (hekat measure of corn) (*part of* **D10,** )

12  **(3)** 1/4 (hekat measure of corn) (*part of* **D10,** )

 ***ḏfḏ*** pupil of the eye

13 **(5)** 1/8 (hekat measure of corn) (*part of* **D10,** )

 ***inḥ*** eye brow(s)

14  **(5)** 1/16 (hekat measure of corn) (*part of* **D10,** )

15  **(5)** 1/32 (hekat measure of corn) (*part of* **D10,** )

16  **(5)** 1/64 (hekat measure of corn) (*part of* **D10,** )

17  **(5)** *figure, image* (*part of* **D10,** )

, , 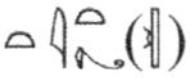 ***tit*** figure, image, shape, design

18  **(5)** *ear*

,  ***msḏr*** ear

 ***msḏrwy*** the two ears

19  **(5)** ***ḫnt*** *nose, smell, face, joy, soft, kind, disobedient*

 ***itnw*** opponent

 ***itnw*** difficulties

,  ***bšt, bšṯ*** be rebellious, rebellion

,  ***bṯn, btn*** be disobedient, defy

,  ***bṯnw, btnw*** defiant man, rebel

D - Parts of the Human Body (cont)

fnḏ, fnd nose

nšp breathe

rš(w) rejoice

ršwt joy

ršršt rejoice

ẖni restrain

ẖnm to smell , to give pleasure

ẖnr restrain

ẖnt face

ẖnt harem, prison, fortress

ẖnty in front of

ẖntš [m] [ḥr] take pleasure [in]

sbt laugh, laughter, mirth

sf be mild

sfn be gentle, kind

sn to smell, kiss

snm greed

sẖnti advance, promote

ssn breathe

ssnt to breathe

šrt nose, nostril

štb rebellion

gꜣw be narrow, constricted, lack (something), short (of breath), deprive (of breath)

gfn, gnf to rebuff

tpiw ox

tpr sniff, breathe

ḏdꜣ fat

D - Parts of the Human Body (cont)

20 (5) (as above)

21 (2) *r*

r, ir to, at, concerning, from, more than, so that, until, according as

r part, 1/320 "**hekat**" measure

r mouth , spell, door, opening, speech, language

r ʿ place, state

r-ʿ end, limit, near, likewise

rʿwy hands or their activity

r pʿt hereditary prince

r pw or

rf (gives emphasis to a command or question)

r m to what end?

rmṯ man, men, mankind

rḫ to know , learn

rn name

rn youbg (animal)

rnn rejoice, exalt

rnn caress

rnn raise (a child), nurse

rnnt wet nurse

r-ntt in-as-much-as

r ʿ ʿ beside, near

rs (used for emphasis) indeed!

rḫ know, learn

rḫ wise man

rḫyt common people

rḫḫy celebrated

rḫt amount, number, knowledge

D - Parts of the Human Body (cont)

rẖt to wash (clothes)

rṯ (used for emphasis with "you")

rṯn (used for emphasis with "you")

rk (used for emphasis with "you")

M6

(5) (see **M6**)

M24

(5) (see **M24**)

M25

(5) (see **M25**)

22

(5)

rwy 2/3

23

(5)

ḫmt rw 3/4

24

(5) (see also **F42**)

spt lip, border (of pool, etc.)

spt shore

ḳmỉ spt reluctant

25

(5) *lips*

spty **lips**

26

(5) *spit, vomit, spew, blood*

bš(ỉ) vomit

psg spit, spit on

rḏw efflux

snf blood

ššdw water drops

ḳꜣꜥ, ḳꜥ spew out

tš spit out

D - Parts of the Human Body (cont)

27 (5) *breast, suckle, nurse, tutor*

- ***mnꜥ*** nurse, suckle
- ***mnꜥy*** male nurse, tutor
- ***mnꜥt*** nurse, foster mother
- ***mnꜥt*** milk cow
- ***mnḏ, mnd*** breast
- ***snḳ*** suckle
- ***sẖr*** to milk
- ***šdi*** suckle, educate

27a (5) (as above)

28 (4) *k3*

- ***k3*** soul, personality, mood, fortune, will (of king)
- ***bk3*** be pregnant
- ***mfk3t*** turquoise
- ***n k3 n*** for the ***k3*** of
- ***ḥk3*** magic
- ***sk3*** to plow
- ***sk3t*** cultivated land
- ***k3w*** food, essence
- ***k3t*** work, construction

29 (5)

- ***k3*** soul, personality, mood, attribute, fortune, will (of king)

30 (5)

- ***nḥb-k3w*** (a serpent deity)

31 (5)

- ***ḥm k3*** "**ka**" priest

D - Parts of the Human Body (cont)

32 (5) *envelop, embrace, open arms*

inḳ envelop, embrace

pgꜣ unfold, spread out, reveal

pgꜣ opening, mouth, entrance

ḥb celebrate a triumph

ḥpt embrace

ẖꜣmi, ẖꜣmi bow down, bend over

ẖꜣmt ẖt, ẖꜣmt ẖt pile of offerings

ḳniw litter, carrying chair

ḳni embrace

33 (5) ***ẖn*** *row, sailor*

ẖni to row, convey (by boat)

ẖnyt sailors

ẖnw sailor

ẖnn destroy, interfere, disturb

ẖnnw turmoil, uproar

ẖnt procession (by water)

ẖnt(y) statue

34 (5) ***ꜥḥꜣ***

ꜥḥꜣ warrior, fight

ꜥḥꜣ [r] , fight [against]

ꜥḥꜣ ḥnꜥ ... r fight with ... against

ꜥḥꜣw arrow

ꜥḥꜣw weapons, arsenal

ꜥḥꜣwty warrior

ꜥḥꜣ-mw sounding pole

ꜥḥꜣt battleground

D - Parts of the Human Body (cont)

ꜥḥꜣt warship

ꜥḥꜣt warriors

ꜥḥꜣt, ꜥḥꜣ tw beware lest

34a (5) (as above)

35 (5) ***n, ḫm*** *not, ignorant*

imi not be (negation)

iḫm sk indestructible

mir do not

n to, for, of, through, in, because, not (etc.)

nn not, cannot, if not, unless, no, without, none, (negates)

nnšm spleen

ḫm be ignorant

ḫm ignorant man

ḫm shrine

smḫ forget

sḫm forget

gnn be soft, weak

(iw)t(y)(i) which not

36 (2) ꜥ (also sometimes used for **D37** through **D34**)

ꜥ arm, hand, region, condition, item

ꜥ warrant, certificate, record

ꜥ bowl, cup

ꜥꜣꜥ valor

ꜥbꜥb to be excited

ꜥbꜥb to appear, to shine

ꜥpr Asiatics

ꜥnḳt (goddess) Anukis

D - Parts of the Human Body (cont)

ꜥḫ brazier

ꜥtḫ to strain (liquid)

m behold

m who?, what?

rdi give, place, cause, grant, track

D59 (5) *ꜥb* (see also under **D36**)

ꜥb horn, archer's bow

ꜥbꜥb threshold

ꜥbt pitchfork

G20 (5) *m* (see **G19**, also with **D37** & **D38**)

mhy be neglectful

G45 (5) *wꜥ*

wꜥw soldier

M27 (5) *šmꜥ* (see also under **M26**)

šmꜥ make music

šmꜥyt chantress, singer

šmꜥw Upper Egypt

O12 (5)

ꜥḥ palace

P7 (5) *ꜥḥꜥ* (see **P6**)

Aa22 (5)

wḏꜥ sever, judge

stḫ (god) Seth (but rarely)

37 (3) *d, mi, m* (see also **D36**)

imi give, place, cause, grant

D - Parts of the Human Body (cont)

m Behold!

mk Behold!

rdi m ib determine

rdi m ḥr command

rdi r tꜣ to land, throw down, neglect

rdi ḥr gs partial, bias, dispose of, kill

rdit n r ḥr s “without neglecting my orders”

hsmḳ wade

di, rdi give, place, cause, grant

ddw Busiris in the delta

38 (3) *mi, m* *give* (see also **D36**)

imi give, place, cause

itm (god) Atum

m behold

m who?, what?

mi(w) waters

mwnf garrison

mfkꜣt turquoise

mm among, therein, there, thence, wherewith

mrkbt chariot

mhy be forgetful, negligent

mhwt family, household

mhr milk jug

mk(i) protect, behold!

mgꜣ skirmisher

mgꜣ young recruits

mḏꜣyw Medjay from Medja

D - Parts of the Human Body (cont)

mḏd hit (a mark), stay on (a path)

n m, in m who, what

39 (3) *offer, present* (see also **D36, D37** and **D38**)

mꜥ in the hand of

rd(i) who causes

ḥnk present

ḥnkw gifts

, ***ḥnkt*** offerings

sḥtpy censer

drp offer food (to), feed (someone)

40 (3) *effort, force, strong action* (use as **A24**, sometimes as **D37**)

ꜣꜣtꜣ Nubian chieftain (?) or his name

ꜣwy present (offerings), announce

[ ] ***iwh [m]*** to load [with]

ꜣẖꜥ to scratch

ꜣsẖ reap

, ***itḥ*** drag, draw, stretch

ꜥbb to knock (on a door)

wꜥw soldier

wdi throw, shoot (an arrow), extend

wdi put, push, emit (a sound)

bḥs to hunt

, , ***pri*** battlefield

pgꜣ unfold, spread out, reveal

ptpt trample down, crush

, ***nbnb*** guard

nẖ to defend, protect, protection

D - Parts of the Human Body (cont)

nḫt strong, victorious, victory, mighty

nḫtw stength, victories

nḫtt victory

ndbw band (a door)

rmrm chastise

ḥ(w)t attack (of falcon)

ḫ3i examine, measure

ḫ3fꜥ capture, grasp

ḫꜥr rage

skw battle, troops

sksk destroy

šꜥd cut down, cut off, cut up

šfꜥ flight

šnš tear up

šr stop up, close

št (tax) assessment

ḳni be strong, prevail over, strong man, strong, dutiful, brave

ḳn brave man

ḳnn superiority

ḳnt strength, bravery, valor

kf uncover, unclothe, strip, deprive, gather, despoil

kfꜥ shoot at

titi crush, trample down

tbtb hoist

tš smash, grind, split

tkk attack, violate (space)

ṯnr eager

drp offer food (to), feed (someone)

D - Parts of the Human Body (cont)

ḏdḥ imprison

41

(5) ***ni*** *arm, shoulder, or movements thereof*

ꜣw length, long, joyful, pleasing

iwḥ [m] to load [with]

iꜣby left

ifd quadruple

ifdy square of cloth

win reject, decline

wnmy right hand

rmn arm, shoulder

rḳ(i) incline

ni reject

niw ostrich

niw bowl

rmn arm, shoulder, side, to carry

rmn (measure of) 1/8 aroura

rmn processional shrine

rmn total

rhn ḥr lean [on], rely [on]

rḳw enemy

rḳi to incline, bend, defy

rḳw tilting, enmity

rḳ ib disaffected one, rebel

ḥ(w)ꜥw short men

ḥsi to praise, favor, sing, honor

ẖms bend (one's back), bow

sg rḥ pacify, make peaceful

sdḥ bring down, humiliate

D - Parts of the Human Body (cont)

kꜥḥ bend the arm, elbow

gbꜣ arm

grḥ cease

dhn [r] promote [to] (position)

42 (5) *place, measure*

imi give, place, cause

mḥ cubit

43 (5) *ḫw*

ḫw fan

ḫwi to protect, exclude

ḫw, ḫwt protection

ḫww evil, baseness

ḫwt sanctuary

sḫwd enrich

44 (5) *control, administer, in front*

ḫrp at the head, in front, control, administer

45 (5) *holy, splendid, clear (a road)*

sḏsr consecrate

tꜣ ḏsr necropolis

ḏsr holy, splendid, private, clear (a road)

ḏsr-imntt Medinet Habu (lit - Western Holy Place)

ḏsrw seclusion, privacy, sanctity

ḏsrw holy place

ḏsr-ḏsrw temple at Deir el Bahri (lit - Holy of Holies)

46 (2) *d* *hand*

ꜣw ḏrt generous (lit - extend a hand)

D - Parts of the Human Body (cont)

wrd tire, be weary destroy

wdỉ put, push, emit (a sound)

bdš faint, languish

rdniw share, portion

ẖrd child

sḳdw sailor, traveler

sdḫ hide

sdg(ỉ) hide

sdgꜣ r hide from, conceal from

sdgw hidden things

d(w) give, place, put, implant, strike

dꜣiw loin cloth

dbḥw measure for offerings

dmỉ fruit dish

dnỉt bowl

ḏws malign

dr subdue, expel, repress

ḏrt, ḏꜣt hand, recite

dgỉ hide

ḏd say, speak

46a (5)

ỉdt fragrance

47 (5) ***ḏrt*** hand (as in **A46**)

48 (5) ***šsp*** palm (linear measure)

49 (5) *seize, grip, grasp, attack*

ꜣmm seize, grip, grasp, attack

ꜣmmt grasp

D - Parts of the Human Body (cont)

ʿrf tie up, pack, envelop, bag

, , ***ẖfʿ*** seize, grip grasp

() ***kfʿw*** warrior

50 (5) ***ḏbʿ*** *finger*

, ***ḏbʿ*** finger, toe, finger width (1/28 cubit)

ḏbʿ 10,000

[] ***ḏbʿ [m]*** point the finger [at]

()() ***ḏbʿw*** reproach

ḏbʿw t, ḏbʿt signet ring

50a (5) *accurate, precise, loyal, rectitude, balance*

ʿḳ3 adjust

ʿḳ3 be precise, accurate

ʿḳ3 equality, level

ʿḳ3w a rope

() ***mty*** precise, straightforward, correct, loyal, trustworthy, regular, customary, exactness

mtr bear witness to

mtrw witnesses

mtt n ib rectitude, affection

m mtt nt ib-f following his heart

mẖ3 to balance, equal

r-ʿḳ3 on a level with

sʿḳ3 set or put in order

51 (5) ***dḳr*** *(finger or toe) nail, measure*

() ***3ẖʿ*** to scratch, scrape, carve, engrave

3ẖʿt scratch, scar

ʿnt finger nail, claw

D - Parts of the Human Body (cont)

wš3 fatten

nḳꜥwt notched sycamore figs

ndb [m] cover [with]

rḳt ib ill will, envy, hostility

ḫ3i measure

ḳ3w grains

ṯ3i take, gird on, rob

ṯ3w take up, seize, rob

, , ***dḳ*** flour, powder

dḳr press, move, expel

, ***dḳr(w)*** fruit

52 (5) ***mt*** *male, phallus* (see also **D53**)

ꜥ3 ass, donkey

iḥ ḥmt cow

wmt be thick

wmt gateway

wmt-ib stout hearted

wmtt fortification, bulwark

mt vein, muscle, vessel of body

mty precise, straightforward, correct, loyal, trustworthy, regular, customary, exactness

mtn reward

mtwt semen, poison

mtnwt reward

mtr bear witness to

mtrw witnesses

mtt n ib rectitude, affection

m mtt nt ib-f following his heart

D - Parts of the Human Body (cont)

ḥ3d lust

ḫmt three, for a third time, treble

ḫmt nw third

ḫmt foretell, expect, think, intend, plan, anticipate

swmt make thick

smtr bear witness to, examine, inquire

k3 bull

k3 n idr best bull (of the herd)

ṯ3y male, man

ṯ3y bull calf

53 (5) ***b3ḥ*** *phallus, its issue, male* (see also **D52**)

imy b3ḥ who is in the presence, who existed before time, ancestor

wsš, wšš urinate

wtt, wtṯ beget

wṯtw offspring

b3ḥ a measure of capacity

b3ḥ foreskin, phallus

bnn beget

m b3ḥ (ʿ) in the presence of

mt strip (of cloth)

mtyt rectitude

mtwt semen, poison

mtmt discuss

mtnwt reward

mtr fame, renown

nk copulate

hi, hy husband

ḥnn phallus

D - Parts of the Human Body (cont)

sti engender, beget

styt procreation

54 (4) *movement, lack of movement*

ꜣb stop, cease, stay, tarry, avoid

ꜣbw cessation

ꜣpd rush forward

ꜣs to hasten, to overtake, quickly, hurry, flow fast

ii come, welcome

iw come

iw f ꜥꜣ f one who rises in rank

ipwty messenger

ifd flee

imy ẖt who follows, accompanies, bodyguard, attendant

ini delay

ir wdf if (something) delays, ie, does not happen

ihm lag, go slowly

is go!

isḳ linger, delay, restrain

yḥ Hey!

ꜥḥꜥ stand up, arise, stand fast, attend, come forth, then

ꜥḥꜥ ḥmsi pass one's life

wꜥr flee, fugitive

wꜥrt flight

wbn walk quickly

wni hasten, hurry, pass by, disregard

wnt neglect

wḫꜣ require, demand

D - Parts of the Human Body (cont)

 ***wsf*** be idle, slack, sluggish

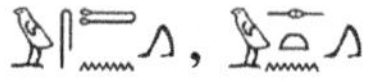 ***wsṯn, wstn*** stride, move freely

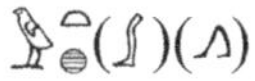 ***wtḫ*** flee

 ***wtḫw*** fugitive

 ***wḏȝ*** proceed, go, set out

 ***wḏỉ*** send forth, set forth

 ***wḏyt*** (military) expedition

 ***wḏȝ*** proceed

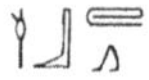 ***wḏb*** turn

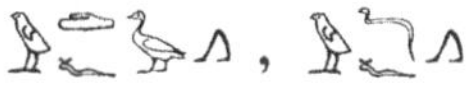 ***wdf, wḏf*** delay, lag, tardy

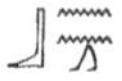 ***bnn*** overflow

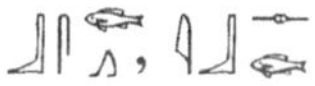 ***bs, ibs*** introduce, enter, influx

 ***bhȝ*** flee

 ***bhȝw*** fugitive

 ***bḥs*** to hunt

 ***prỉ*** go forth

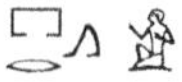 ***pry*** hero, champion

 ***pr ʿ*** energetic, activity

 ***prw*** excess, surplus

 ***prw*** motion, procession, result

 ***pr r ḫȝ*** go forth abroad

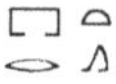 ***prt*** procession

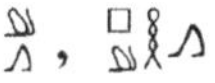 ***pḥ*** reach, attain, finish, attack, end by

 ***pḥrr*** run

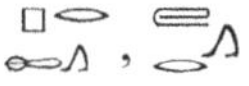 ***pḫr*** turn, go round, serve

 ***psḫ*** be in disorder, distraught

 ***ptpt*** trample down, crush

 ***ptḫ*** overthrow

pd kneel, run

fḫ loose, release, cast off, destroy, depart**)**

ftft leap

mi come (imperative)

mnmn move about, be disturbed

m ḫt after, afterward, accompanying

ms bring, present, bring away booty, extend (aid), take aim

nftft leap

nmtt step, walk

nmttw steps, walks

nr charge (an enemy)

nhp to care (for)

nš supplant, drive away, expel

nš ḥr supplant, drive away [from]

rwi [r] cease, make to cease, depart [from]

hꜣ Ha, Ho

hꜣi come down, go down, descend, grasp (meaning), fall, charge down, drip, drop, tackle, befall, attack

hꜣb [n] [ḥr] send [to] [about]

hb enter, penetrate into, travel

hsmḳ wade

hdhd (army) charge

ḥf range (of game)

ḥḥy seek, search for, be missing

ḫꜣḫ hasten

ḫm wild

ḫni alight, halt

D - Parts of the Human Body (cont)

ḫns traverse

ḫntš walk about

ḫt throughout, pervading, through

ẖꜥm, ḫꜥm approach

ḫn approach, draw near

sꜣi linger

sꜣḥ approach, reach, arrive at, kick

sꜣsꜣ repel, force (boat), overthrow

sꜥr make to ascend, offer up

swꜣ pass by, escape

swtwt promenade, walk around, journey

sbi go, pass, send, attain, conduct, load

spr approach, arrive, reach

spri cause to miss, expel

sn to open

sni to surpass, pass by

snhp spur on, start

shꜣi send down, cause to fall

sḫs to run, hurry

sḫsḫ to run fast

sḫty run

sš spread out, pass

stp leap up, over leap

stkn cause to approach, bring on

stp leap up, over leap

sdgi [r] to hide, conceal [from]

sdgw hidden thing

šm go

D - Parts of the Human Body (cont)

šrš hurry

kf uncover, unclothe, strip, deprive, gather

gst speed

thw transgressor

, , , [ ] *tši [r]* be missing, stray [from]

tkn approach, draw near, meet

tkk attack, violate (space)

ṯiṯi trot, crush, trample on

, *ṯsi* go up

dḳr press, move, expel

ḏꜥ to spear, harpoon

( )( ) *ḏꜥr* search for

M18 (5) *i* *come and related words*

ii come, welcome

iyt mishap, harm, trouble, wrong

N40 (5) *š* (implies motion)

šm go

nnšm spleen

O35 (5) *s* (implies motion, see **O35**)

T32 (5) *sšm* (guide, lead, see **T32**)

sšm guide, lead

, , *sšmw, sšmy* divine shape, form, statue

V15 (5) *ṯ* (implies motion)

, , , *iṯ(i), it(i)* carry off, seize, take possession of, remove, arrest, spend (time)

iṯw thief

D - Parts of the Human Body (cont)

W25  (5) ***in*** (implies motion)

 ,  ,  ***in(i)*** bring, remove, carry off, bring about, overcome, reach

 ***inyt*** refrain (of song)

 ,  ***inw*** produce, quarry, gifts, tribute

 ***inw*** matting

 ***inw*** pattern, model

55  (5) *backward, turn back, retreat, reverse*

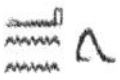 ***ʿnn*** turn back

 ***msnḥ*** turn backward

 ***ḥm*** flee, retire, retreat

 ***ḥs*** turn back

 ***ḫtḫt*** be reversed, retreat

 ***sbḫꜣ*** cause to retreat

 ,  ***tnm*** go astray

56  (5) ***pds, wʿr, sbḳ, gḥ, gḥs*** *leg, thigh, knee, shank*

 ***ʿꜣg*** flog, beat the feet of

 ***iry rdwy*** attendant

 ***isḳ*** linger, delay, restrain

 ***wʿr*** flee, fugitive

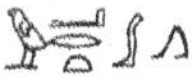 ***wʿrt*** flight

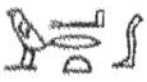 ***wʿrt*** leg, shank

 ,  ***wʿrt*** administrative district

 ***wʿrtw*** district official

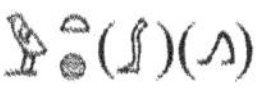 ***wtḫ*** flee

 ***wtḫw*** fugitive

 ***bḥs*** to hunt

 ***btꜣ*** run

D - Parts of the Human Body (cont)

 ***pd, pꜣd*** knee

 ***pd*** kneel, run

 ***pds*** box

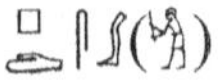 ***pds*** stamp flat

 ***pdswt*** Delta dunes

 ***mꜣst*** thigh, lap

 ***mnt*** thigh

 ***rd*** foot

 ***rdw*** stairway

 ***rdwy*** the two feet

 ***ẖnd*** tread

 ***ẖnd*** lower part, calf (of leg)

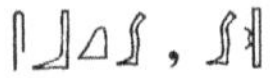 ***sbḳ*** leg, calf, splendid, precious

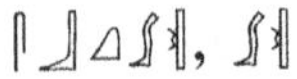 ***sbḳ*** excellent, successful

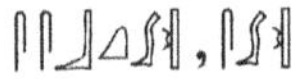 ***ssbḳ*** honor

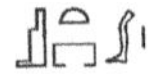 ***st-rd*** rank

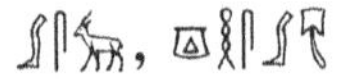 ***gḥ, gḥs*** gazelle

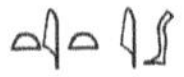 ***titỉ*** crush, trample down

 ***tp ḥr mꜣst*** in mourning (id)

 ***tp-rd*** instructions, rules, principles

 ***tpt-rd*** task

 ***thw*** transgressor

 ***tšỉ [r]*** be missing, stray [from]

 ***dgꜣ*** to walk

57  **(5)** *mutilate, execute, cheat, damage*

 ***ỉꜣt, ỉꜣt*** be mutilated, missing

 ***ỉꜣṯw*** place of execution

 ***nkn*** damage

D - Parts of the Human Body (cont)

 ***sjꜣt*** purloin, cheat

,  ***sjꜣty*** cheat

58  (2) ***b***

 ***biꜣw*** wonders, marvels

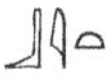 ***bit*** vase

,  ***bw*** place, position

  ***bw bin*** misery

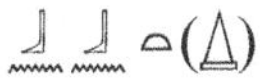 ***bnbnt*** pyramidion

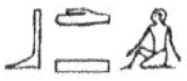 ***bdš*** faint, languish

,  ***b(ꜣ)gi*** be remiss, slack

 ***bin*** bad, miserable, act evilly

 ***bḳ*** be hostile

 ***snb*** health, healthy

59  (5) ***ꜥb***

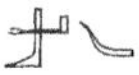 ***ꜥb*** horn , cup

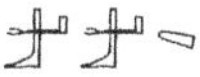 ***ꜥbꜥb*** threshold

60  (5) ***wꜥb***

,  ***wꜥb*** pure, clean

 ***wꜥb*** be pure, clean

 ***wꜥb*** priest

 ***wꜥbw*** clean clothes, sacred robe

 ***wꜥbt*** tomb, sanctuary, embalming place

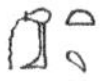 ***wꜥbt*** meat offering

 ***swꜥb*** purify, cleanse

S13  **(5)** (see **S13**)

 ***nbi*** gild, fashion

D - Parts of the Human Body (cont)

61  (5) ***s3ḥ***

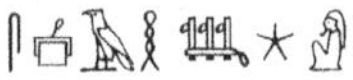,  ***s3ḥ*** (constellation) Orion

,  ***s3ḥ*** grant, endowment

,  ***s3ḥ*** grant, endowment (of land)

, ,  ***s3ḥ*** land grant

, 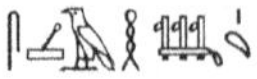 ***s3ḥ*** toe

, 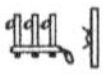,  ***s3ḥ*** approach, reach, arrive at, kick

 ***s3ḥ*** dependant

 ***s3ḥw*** neighbors, dependents

,  ***s3ḥt*** neighborhood

[]  ***[m]-s3ḥt*** [in] the neighborhood

62  (5) (as above)

63  (5) (as above)

E - Mammals

1 (5) *cattle, bull, oxen*

iw3 ox

iryt dairy cow

iḥ ox, bull

iḥ ḥmt cow

idr herd of cattle

idt cow

wšb bull

wndw short horned cattle

wdww wandering herds

mnʿt milk cow

mnmnt cattle

mr-wr Menevis bull

mdt stalled cattle

nḥbw yoked oxen

ng bull

rny calf

ḥpw Apis bull

ḥtr team of oxen

s3bt dappled cow

sḫtyw class of cattle

k3 bull

kmy(t) herd (of cattle)

k3 n idr best bull (of the herd)

tpiw ox

ṯnwt number of cattle

1a (5) ***ḥpw*** sacred bull

E - Mammals (cont)

2 (5) *bull*

pry champion (ferocious) bull

, , ***smꜣ*** fighting bull

kꜣ bull (pharaoh)

kꜣ n idr bull of the herd

, ***kꜣ nḫt*** strong bull (pharaoh)

3 (5) *short horned cattle, calf*

wnḏw short horned cattle

rny calf

ṯꜣy bull calf

4 (5)

, ***ḥsꜣt*** sacred cow

5 (5) *show solicitude*

, ***ꜣms*** show solicitude

6 (5) *horse, stallion*

ib(ꜣ)r stallion

rnp colt

ḥtr team of horses, chariotry

, , ***ssm(t)*** horse

7 (5) *ass*

, ***ꜥꜣ*** ass

8 (5) ***ib*** *small cattle, flocks, goats*

ib suppose, imagine

ib kid

ibi be thirsty

ibw refuge

E - Mammals (cont)

ibḥ priest who performs libations

ibḥw one who performs libations

ibt thirst

ʿwt flock, herd, goats

bḥs calf

mnmnt herds

8a

(5) (as above)

9

(5) ***iw***

iw dog

iw wrong, crime

iw complaint

iw(y) one without a boat

iwyt street, house, area, sanctuary

iwyt wrongdoing

iwʿ thigh (of beef), femur

iwʿ inherit, inherit from

iwʿyt garrison, soldiery, troops

iwʿ [m] reward [with]

iwʿw heir

iwʿw ring

iwʿt heiress

iwʿt heritage, inheritance

iwnn sanctuary

iwnyt hall of columns

iwr conceive, become pregnant

iwh [m] to load [with]

iwḥ to moisten, water, irrigate

E - Mammals (cont)

iwḥw inundation

iwsw balance, scale

iwtyw corruption

iwtn ground, floor

iwd to separate

iwdt separation

niwiw be glad

r-iwd ... r between ... and

siw [r] bring a complaint [against]

siwḥ rob

siwḥ inundated

sft sacrifice

10 (5) *ram, sheep*

ʿwt ḥḏt sheep (white flock)

bꜣ ram

ḫnmw god Khnum

sr sheep

11 (5) (as above)

12 (5) *pig*

rri pig

rrt sow

šꜣi pig

13 (5) *cat*

miw, mit cat

14 (5) *dog*

iw dog

E - Mammals (cont)

ṯsm hound

15 (5) *Anubis*

ỉnpw Anubis

ỉnp(w) crown prince, royal child

ḥry sštꜣ "He who is over the secrets"

16 (5) (as above)

17 (5) *jackal, dignitary, worthy*

ḥtt hyena

sꜣb jackal

sꜣb dignitary, worthy

18 (5) *Wepwawet*

wp-wꜣwt (the god) Wepwawet

19 (5) (as above)

20 (5) *turmoil, confusion, Seth*

nbwy the Two Lords (Seth and Horus)

nmꜥ [n] show partiality [to], question

nšny rage, storm, foul weather, disaster

ẖnn destroy, interfere, disturb

ẖnnw turmoil

swh [n] to boast [about]

shꜣ confusion

stẖ, stš god Seth

21 (5) *turmoil, rage, storm*

nšnỉ rage, storm, foul weather, disaster

hmhmt roaring, war cry, squawking

swh [n] to boast [about]

E - Mammals (cont)

22 (5) *lion*

mꜣi lion

mꜣ-ḥsꜣ lion

23 (5) ***rw, šnʿ*** *lion, actions of a lion* (used for "L" in foreign words)

ꞽtrw river

pꜣḫt a lion goddess

mšrw evening

rꞽt side

rw lion

rwyt judgment hall

rwty lion's den

rwty the Two-lion god

ršwt joy

ḫꜣrw Khor (in Canaan)

ḫꜣrw one from Khor

ḫnrw reins

ẖrw low lying land

šnʿ hold back, repel, deter, turn back

šnʿ storage magazine

šspw sphinx

krr Gerar (in Syria)

ḏsrw holy place

23a **nb** image

24 (5) *panther, leopard*

ꜣby panther, leopard

25 (5) *hippopotamus*

ḫꜣb hippopotamus

E - Mammals (cont)

,  ***ḏb, ḏib*** hippopotamus

26  (5) *elephant*

, ,  ***ꜣbw*** elephant

,  ***ꜣbw*** Elephantine (UE)

,  ***idr*** herd of elephants

27  (5) ***sr*** *foretell, challenge*

 ***sr*** foretell, make known

 ***sr-ꜥḥꜣ*** challenge to battle

 ***srwt*** prophecies

28  (5) *oryx, greed*

 ***ꜣfꜥ*** greed, be greedy

,  ***mꜣḥḏ*** oryx

 ***ẖnm*** herd

29  (5) *gazelle*

,  ***gḥs*** gazelle

30  (5) *ibex*

,  ***niꜣw*** ibex

31  (5) *goat, rank, dignity, noble*

,  ***ꜥnẖt*** goat

 ***msbb*** to turn

,  ***sꜥḥ*** be noble, rank, dignity, nobleman, worthy

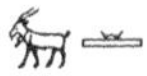 ***sꜥḥ*** to ennoble

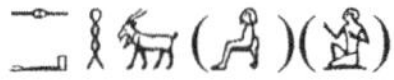, ,  ***sꜥḥ*** (deceased) noble

 ***sꜥḥ*** mummy

32  (5) *baboon, monkey, anger*

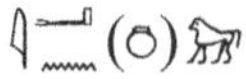,  ***iꜥn*** baboon, sacred baboon

E - Mammals (cont)

ḳnd be furious, angry

ky monkey

32a (5) *baboon, Thoth*

bnty two baboons that greet the morning sun

ḏḥwty (god) Thoth

33 (5) *monkey*

gf monkey

34 (4) ***wn*** (see also **M42** and **Z11**)

iw wn there is

ꜥwn defraud, rapacious, covetous, despoil

ꜥwnt stick, club

wn open, open up, rip open

wn fault, failing, blame

wni hasten, hurry, pass by, disregard

wnw Hermopolis (Ashmunen) (Upper Egypt)

wnwn sway, travel about

wnwt hour, priestly duties

wnwt priesthood

wnwt(y) hour watcher, astrologer

wnpw triumph

wnf be glad, happy

wnm eat

wn-mꜣꜥ truth, reality

wnn exist, be

wnt , ***wnnt*** indeed, really

wn ḥr instructed, expert

wn ḥr n enlightenment is given to

E - Mammals (cont)

wnḫ be clad that

wns sledge

wnš jackal or similar animal

wnt neglect

pwnt Punt (Somalia)

ḥwn youthful, youth, vigor, be young, refreshed, child, young man

swn perish

swnt arrow

swnt sale

sḫꜥt hare

ddwn a Nubian god

F - Parts of Mammals

1  (5) (also use as **E1**)

 ***iḥ*** ox, bull

 ***k3*** ox

2  (5) *characteristics of bulls*

 ,  ***ḏnd*** rage

 ***ẖpn*** fat

3  (5) ***3t*** *characteristics of hippos*

 ***3sb*** fierce, glowing

 ,  ***3t*** instant, moment

 ***3t*** striking power, attack

 ***tp-i3t*** due time (to act)

4  (5) *fore, front*

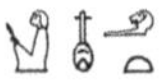 , 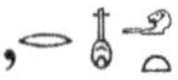 ***iry nfr ḥ3t*** keeper of the diadem

 ***imy ḥ3t*** who (which) is in front, prototype, pattern, mold, example

 ***imt ḥ3t f*** uraeus

 ***imyw-ḥ3t*** ancestors

 ***ꜥš-ḥ3t*** pilot

 ***m3-sḥ3t*** bow

 ,  ***r-ḥ3t*** mouth (of river)

 ,  ,  ***ḥ3wty*** the foremost

 ,  ***ḥ3t*** front, fore, forward, van , foremost

 [] ***ḥ3t -ꜥ [m]*** beginning [of]

[][][]  ***[m] [r] [ẖr] ḥ3t*** in front of, before

 ***ḥ3ty*** breast, heart

 ***ḥ3ty-ꜥ*** the finest of

 () ***ḥ3ty -ꜥ*** local prince, mayor

F - Parts of Mammals (cont)

ḥ3twy-ʿ local princes, mayors

ḥ3tt prow rope

ḫr ḥ3t formerly

5 (5) ***šs3***

bḫnt pylon

sš3 prayer

šs3 be skilled

šs3w prescription

ḏd3 fat

6 (5) ***šs3*** (as above)

7 (5) *worth, dignity, majesty, ram's head*

3tf be crowned

ḫnmw (god) Khnum

šfyt worth, dignity, majesty

šfšft ram's head, respect, awe

šft ram headed figure (Amun)

8 (5) (as above)

9 (5) *strength*

b3 leopard skin

pḥty strength, power

10 (5) *neck, throat, swallow, parched*

ʿm to swallow, know

ʿm ib to faint, lose consciousness

ʿm ib ḥr be thoughtless, neglectful

nḏ3 be parched, stifled

ḫḫ throat

F - Parts of Mammals (cont)

ḥtyt throat

sꜥm to swallow down, wash down (food)

11 (5) (as above)

12 (5) ***wsr***

wsr be powerful, wealthy, power, wealth

wsr wealthy man

wsr oar

wsrt neck

swsr make powerful

12a (as above)

13 (5) ***wp, ip***

ipwty messenger

ipt mission, message, occupation

wpi divide, open, judge, discern, distinguish

wpy decision

wp-wꜣwt Wepwawet (the wolf god)

wpw ḥr except, but

wpwt message

wpwty messenger, agent

wpš strew, scatter

wpt specification

wpt top knot

wpt st specifically

wpt brow, top (of head), beginning, vertex

wpt-rnpt New Year's Day

wpt tꜣ earth's beginning, the extreme south

swsḫ widen, extend, enlarge

F - Parts of Mammals (cont)

14 (5)

wpt-rnpt New Year's Day

15 (5) (as above)

16 (5) ***ʿb*** *horn*

ʿʿb to comb

ʿb horn

ʿb unite

ʿbʿ boast, exaggerate

ʿbw victims

sfḫt-ʿbw "The seven Horned"

db horn, wing (of the army)

ḥn(w)t horn

m ʿb together with, in the company of

17 (5) ***ʿbw, wʿb***

ʿbw purification, offerings

ʿbw r breakfast

swʿb cleanse

18 (5) ***bḥ, ḥw, bi*** *tooth, bite, laugh*

ibḥ tooth, tusk

wšʿ bite, chew

biꜣ firmament, heaven

biꜣy of bronze

biꜣw mine

biꜣ(y)t wonder, marvel

bit character, qualities

bḥs calf

F - Parts of Mammals (cont)

bḥdt Behdet (LE), Edfu (UE)

bḥdty he of Behdet

psḥ bite

mꜣ-ḥsꜣ lion

, ***nḥdt*** tooth ***nḥdt*** tooth

ndḥt, nḥdt tusk

hw god of authoritative utterance

()()()(), , ***ḥw*** food, sustenance

sbḥ cry

, ***sbt*** laugh, laughter, mirth

, ***tḥw*** rejoice, exultation, joy

dbḥw requirements, necessities

, ***dbḥw*** measure for offerings

dbḥt necessaries

, ***dbḥt*** funerary meal

dbḥt-ḥtp altar

19 (5) *jaw*

ꜥrt jaw

20 (5) ***ns*** *tongue, taste, mouth, overseer*

, ***imy r*** overseer

ny-sw he belongs to

, ***ns*** tongue

ns flame

nswt flame, fire

nsb lick

nsr burn, blaze

nsrt flame

nsrt (goddess) Neshert, uraeus, royal serpent

F - Parts of Mammals (cont)

ns-sḏꜣwty chief treasurer

nst seat, throne

nst cut (?)

nsty a type of bread

ntb be parched

snk tongue

st-ns speech

dp taste

dpty an offering

21 (5) ***idn, sḏm*** *hear, deaf, obey, serve, leaf shaped*

idi be deaf

idn replace, serve instead of, proxy

idn serve as lieutenant commander

idnw deputy, substitute, overseer

ꜥnẖwy two ears

msḏr ear

mtmt discuss

snktkt gossip

sẖi be deaf

sḏm to hear, obey

sḏm eye paint

sḏm ꜥš servant

sḏmi judge

sḏmt ꜥš female servant

ḏrḏ tree leaf

22 (5) ***pḥ, kꜣ*** *extreme, rear*

ꜥrt hind quarters

pḥ reach, attain, finish, attack, end by

F - Parts of Mammals (cont)

, ***pḥwy*** hind quarters, back, rearguard, end, stern

pḥwy-r down to

pḥwyt rectum

, , ***pḥwyt*** stern-rope (of ship)

, , , , ***pḥww*** marshlands, far north, distant marshlands, outer limits, ends of the earth

pḥww m northward to

pḥt r ending at

, , ***pḥty*** strength, power

pḥt-r northwards to, ending at

m3-spḥw stern

spḥ attain

, ***kf*** uncover, unclothe, strip, deprive, gather

kf3 rear (of bird), bottom (of a pot)

, ***kf3-ib*** discreet, trustworthy, careful

[ ], [ ] ***kf3-ib [ḥr]*** trustworthy [in]

m-kf(3)t "indeed"

23 (5) *foreleg, arm, power*

, ***ḫpš*** foreleg, thigh, arm, strength, power

ḫpš strong arm

ḫpš Great Bear constellation

m-ḫpš acquire by one's own strength

msḫtyw Great Bear constellation

stpt choice

24 (5) (as above)

25 (5) ***wḥm***

, ***wḥm*** ass

F - Parts of Mammals (cont)

wḥm repeat

m wḥm (ʿ) a second time, again

wḥm ʿnḫ life (living) after death

wḥmw herald, reporter

wḥmwty-f there will never be his like again

wḥmt hoof

26 (5) *ẖn*

ʿẖnwty inner chambers, audience hall

mẖnty ferry boat operator

[m]-ẖnw [in the] interior, inside

ẖn approach, draw near

ẖn tent

ẖnw royal residence

ẖnw interior

ẖnw stream, brook

ẖnw-ʿwy embrace

ẖnwtyw skin clad people

ẖnt skin

ẖnt burial chamber

27 (5) *mammal, skin, hide, rug, leather* (see also **F28**)

ỉpt festival of the 12th month

ỉnm skin

ỉkm shield

wnš wolf, jackal or similar animal

bꜣ leopard skin

pnw mouse

mꜣỉ lion

F - Parts of Mammals (cont)

miw, mit cat

mmy giraffe

msḥ crocodile

mss corselet

mskꜣ skin, hide, rug

niꜣw ibex

rsw sentry, vigilance

hꜣrt herds (of animals)

hnn deer

ẖꜣwt (animal) hide

ẖnrw reins

ẖnwtyw skin clad people

ẖnm herd

ẖnt skin

šꜣk bag

šsm leather roll

šdw water skin, cushion, mat

gf monkey

dḥr(i) skin, hide, leather

ḏḥrw leather lacings

28 (5) *ꜣb* *hide* (see also **F27** and **U23**)

ꜣbḏw Abydos

sꜣb variegated, dappled

sꜣbt dappled cow

sꜣb šwt variegated feathers (of Horus)

šꜣk bag

F - Parts of Mammals (cont)

29 (5) *st* *pierce, target*

mgꜣ skirmisher

stꞽ pour

stꞽ stare at

stꞽ pierce

stꞽ [m] kindle, set fire [to]

stꞽ [r] shoot [at]

stꞽ [r] to spear, thrust [into]

styt procreation

stw target

stwt rays

stt (goddess) Satis

sṯt, stꞽ engender, beget

30 (5) *šd*

ꞽšd **"ished"** tree (of life?)

wšd address, question

mšdt ford

sšd head band, bandage

sšd don a head band

sšd lightning flash

sšd gleam, glitter, flash

šd artificial lake

šdꞽ recite, read out loud

šdꞽ suckle, educate

šdꞽ draw forth, rescue, educate, dig, dig out

šdy ditch

šdyt pool, plot of land

šdyt rubble

F - Parts of Mammals (cont)

šdw water skin, cushion, mat

šdw waterfowl

šdw, šdwt plot of ground

šd-ḥrw disturbance

šd-r public proclamation

šdt Medinet el Fayyum, Crocodilopolis

31 (5)*ms*

ꜣms club, mace, royal scepter, staff, wield (an ***ꜣms***)

ꜣms show solicitude

ꜣms lie, falsehood

iw ms misstatement

ims ib pleasant, kindly disposed (to)

(m) hỉ ms approaching in a humble manner

ms born of

ms bouquet

msỉ give birth, form, fashion

msy last

msyt make a festival

msyt supper, evening meal

mswt birth

mswt young children or animals

mswtt girl child

msbb to turn

msnw harpooner, hippopotamus hunter

msnḥ turn backward

msẖn abode of the gods

msẖtyw adze

msẖtyw Great Bear constellation

F - Parts of Mammals (cont)

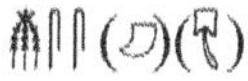 ***mss*** corselet

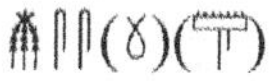 ***mss*** tunic

***mss*** totter

 ***msḳ*** leather

 ***msḳt*** the Milky Way

 ***msk3*** hide, skin

 ***mski*** rumor

 ***msktw*** armlet

 ***mst*** fox skin apron

 ***mstiwty*** descendant of a god

 ***mstw*** offspring

 ***mstpt*** funeral bier

,  ***msdmt, msḏmt*** kohl, black eye paint

,  ***msḏi, msdi*** to hate

 ***msḏr*** ear

 ***msḏḏt*** what is hateful

,  ***hi ms*** approaching in a humble manner

,  ***ṯms*** be besmeared

32  (2) ẖ

 ***ẖꜥm*** approach (with hostile intent)

 ***ẖꜥḳ*** shave

 ***ẖwt*** bodies, bellies

 ***ẖp3*** navel, umbilical

 ***ẖpw*** sculptured reliefs

 ***ẖpn*** fat

 ***ẖms*** bend (one's back)

 ***ẖrd*** child

F - Parts of Mammals (cont)

ẖsy weak, feeble, vile

ẖt body, belly

n ẖt.f of his body

ẖt body of people, generation

ẖdb kill

33 (5) *sd*

ḥb sd "**Sed**" festival, jubilee

sd jubilee

sd tail

sdty a title

33a (5) *sd* (see previous)

34 (5) *heart, wish*

ꜣwt ib joy, happiness (lit -wide heart)

iꜥi ib satisfy (one's) desire, appetite, wrath

ib heart, seat of intelligence

ib wish

ims ib pleasant, kindly disposed (to)

ꜥm ib to faint, lose consciousness

ꜥm ib ḥr be thoughtless, neglectful

wꜣḥ-ib patient, well disposed

wmt-ib stout hearted

mr ib n be sorry for

mr ḥr ib n be displeasing to

mḥ-ib be trustworthy, trusted

nḏm ib joyful

rḳt ib ill will, envy, hostility

rdi ib m-sꜣ be anxious about

F - Parts of Mammals (cont)

rdi ib ḫnt pay attention to

rdi m ib determine)

ḥ3ty heart

ḫnti-ib glad of heart

[m] ḥr(y)-ib [in] the midst of

ḫrt-ib wish, desire

ḫ3kw-ib disaffected, rebel

s3wi-ib to gladden

snk-ib haughtiness

st-ib affection (lit - place in the heart)

kf3-ib be discreet, trustworthy, careful

ṯ3-ib able

di m ib-f determine

35 (5) ***nfr***

iry nfr ḫ3t keeper of the diadem

wn-nfr Osiris

m m3ʿw nfr with a good wind, with good dispatch

mn-nfr Memphis (LE)

nfr good, perfect, beautiful

nfr good, perfect, beautiful, good fortune

nfr crown of Upper Egypt

nfryt end, bottom, until

nfrw beauty, perfection, goodness, back of, end of

nṯr nfr (the) perfect god

nfr-ḥḏt crown of Upper Egypt

snfr make perfect, make beautiful, embellish

F - Parts of Mammals (cont)

36 (5) *smꜣ*

smꜣ lung

smꜣ unite

smꜣyt association, confederation

smꜣyt consort

smꜣt union

smꜣt-ʿ an offering

smꜣt-ʿꜣt a fabric

37 (5) *sm* *back*

iꜣt back

idw pestilence

psḏ back, spine

sm succor

šʿd cut down, cut off, cut up

37a (5) (as above)

38 (5) (as above)

39 (5) *back, spinal cord, venerated state*

imꜣẖ spinal cord

imꜣẖ venerated state

psḏ back, spine

40 (5) *ꜣw*

ꜣwy arouse

ꜣw deceased (lit - extended)

ꜣw death

ꜣw length, long, joyful, pleasing

ꜣwi be long, stretch out, expanded

F - Parts of Mammals (cont)

 ***ꜣwi*** extend, stretch out

 ***ꜣwt ib*** joy, happiness (lit -wide heart)

 ***ꜣwi, ꜣwy***
extend, announce, arouse, present (an offering)

 ***ꜣwy*** announce

 ***ꜣwḥ*** do violence

 ***ꜣw ḥr*** farsighted

 ***ꜣwt*** length (of time)

 ***ꜣwt*** long knife

 ***ꜣwt , ꜣwt ꜥ*** gifts, offerings

 ***ꜣw ḏrt*** generous (lit - extend a hand)

 ***fꜣw*** magnificence

 ***fꜣw*** food supplies

 ***mꜣwt*** shaft

 ***niꜣw*** ibex

 ***nꜥw*** breeze

 ***r ꜣw*** Turah (limestone quarry site)

 ***r ꜣw-f*** entire, all

 ***sꜣwi*** lengthen, prolong

 ***sꜣwy ḥr*** keep an eye on

 ***sꜣwi ib*** to gladden (lit - to lengthen the heart)

41  (5) *šꜥ back*

 ***psd*** back, spine

 ***šꜥt*** blood lust, slaughter,
ferocity

 ***šꜥd*** cut off, cut up, cut down

42  (5) *spr rib*

 ***spr*** rib

F - Parts of Mammals (cont)

spr approach, arrive, reach

sprw, sprty petitioner

43 (5) *ribs*

spḥt ribs of beef

44 (5) ***iwʿ, isw*** *thigh, femur*

iwʿ thigh (of beef), femur

iwʿ inherit

iwʿt heritage

isw exchange, repay, reward

iswty representative

(m) (r) isw in return for

swt leg of beef, tibia

45 (5) *cow, womb*

idt cow

idt vulva, womb

46 (5) ***pẖr, bdn*** *intestine, go round, in the midst of*

wḏb, wdb turn

wḏb sandbank, shore, river bank

wḏb-ʿ desist, gain composure

pẖr turn, go round

pẖr wr Euphrates River

pẖrt remedy, medicine

pẖrt frontier guard

pẖrty traveler

spẖr circulate

spẖr register, copy

sḳb double

F - Parts of Mammals (cont)

ḳꜣb intestine

ḳꜣb interior, middle

ḳ(ꜣ)b to double back

ṯs saying, utterance

ḏbn helmet

ḏbn go round

ḏbnt circuit (of the ocean)

46a (5) (as above)

47 (5) (as above)

47a (5) (as above)

48 (5) (as above)

49 (5) (as above)

50 (5) ***spẖr*** write out, copy

51 (5) *flesh, limb, parts of the body*

ꜣst (goddess) Isis

iwꜣ beef

iwf meat

imꜣḫ spinal cord

idt vulva, womb

ꜥt limb

wꜥbt meat offering

, ***wbnw*** wound

wri portion

wsir (god) Osiris

bꜣḥ foreskin, phallus

bꜥnt neck

F - Parts of Mammals (cont)

pꜥt patricians, mankind

psḏ back, spine

, ***pd, pꜣd*** knee

pḥwy hind quarters, back, rearguard, end, stern

pḥwyt rectum

mist liver

mt vein, muscle, vessel of body

nḥbt neck, shoulder

ns tongue

rmn arm, shoulder, side, to carry

ḥꜥ flesh

, ***ḥꜥw*** members, body

ḥꜥw self

ḥꜥw-nṯr the king (lit - flesh of the god)

ḫpdw buttocks

ḫnd lower part, calf (of leg)

, ***sꜣḥ*** toe

spr rib

()(), ***stpt*** choice

šnbt breast

ḳꜣb intestine, interior, middle

, ***kns*** vagina

ḏrw side

() ***ḏrt, ḏꜣt*** hand

52 (5)

, ***ḥs*** excrement

F - Parts of Mammals (cont)

80  (5)

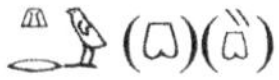 ***ẖrwy*** testicles

81  (*symbol of Crocodilopolis*)

 ***šdty*** "He of Crocodilopolis"

82  (5) *deer*

 ***ẖnn*** deer

G - Birds

1  **(2)** ***ȝ*** vulture (easily confused with **G4**)

 ***ȝȝ*** ruin(s)

 [] ***ȝbḫ [m]*** mingle [with]

 ***ȝpd*** goose, bird, fowl

 ***ȝfʿ*** greed, be greedy

 ***ȝm*** burn

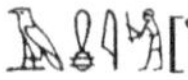[] ***ȝmi [ḥr]*** mix, compound [with]

 ***ȝmm*** seize, grip

 ***ȝmmt*** grasp

 ***ȝhw*** pain, trouble

 ***ȝhd*** be feeble, faint

,  ***ȝḥt*** field, arable land, earth

,  ***ȝḫw*** sunshine

,  ***ȝḥt*** field

 ***ȝḫʿ*** scratch

 ***ȝs*** hasten, overtake, quickly

 ***ȝsḫ*** reap

 ***ȝḳ*** perish

 ***ȝkr*** (god) Aker

 ***ȝd*** be aggressive, angry

()[],  ***ȝtp [m], ȝtp*** load [with]

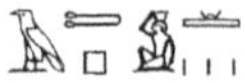 ***ȝtpw*** load

2  **(5)** ***ȝȝ***

 ***mȝȝ*** see

3  **(5)** ***mȝ***

 ***smȝwy*** renew, renovate

G - Birds (cont)

4 (5) ***tyw*** (easily confused with **G1**)

iꜣbtyw Easterners

iꜣbtyw the east of

iwtyw corruption

imntyw westerners (deceased)

irtyw mourning

itywn(y) "welcome!"

ꜥntyw myrrh

ꜥḥwtyw tenet farmers, field laborers

bwytyw abominated ones

bšttyw rebels

pwntyw the people of Punt

mꜣꜥtyw just man

mḥtyw northerners

mstiwty descendant of a god

ḥꜣtwy-ꜥ local princes, mayors

ḥmwwtyw craftsmen

ḫꜣstyw foreigners, desert dwellers

ḫbstyw bearded ones of Punt

ḫntyw tenants

ḫntyw-tꜣ Southerners

ẖrtyw-nṯr necropolis workmen

ḫtyw threshing floor

ẖnwtyw skin clad people

sḏꜣwtyw treasurers

knmtyw those who dwell in darkness

tisw stick, staff

G - Birds (cont)

ḏꜣytyw opponents

ḏrtyw ancestors

5 **(5)** ***ḥr, ḥrw*** *(god) Horus*

wꜣwt Roads of Horus

ḥr (falcon god) Horus

6 **(5)** *falcon*

bik falcon

bik "Falcon" ship

7 **(5)** *Horus, god, king*

i, wi I, me (king)

iꜥḥ moon

ipwty messenger

imn Amun (same use with other gods)

imsti "**Imseti**" one of the sons of Horus

ity sovereign

ꜥḫm divine image

nbwy the Two Lords (Seth and Horus)

nbwy the Two Lords (Seth and Horus)

nsw king

nṯr god, divine

ḥꜣ (desert god) Ha

ḥw royal decree

ḥr (falcon god) Horus

ḫnsw the tenth month, (moon god) Khonsu

ḫnty-ḫty the eleventh month

ḫnmw (god) Khnum

G - Birds (cont)

7a (5) ***ʿnty*** god of 12th nome of Upper Egypt

7b (5) (as above)

R13 (5) *right side, west*

imn right, right handed

imnt west

imntyw westerners (deceased)

O10 (5)

ḥt-ḥr (goddess) Hathor

8 (5)

ḥr n nbw Golden Horus (king's title)

9 (5) *Ra Horakhty*

rʿ-ḥr-ꜣḫty (god) Ra Horakhty

10 (5) *Sokar*

ḥnw (god) Sokar's bark

skr (god) Sokar

11 (5) *divine image, breast*

ʿšm, ʿḫm, ʿḫm divine image

šnbt breast

gmḥsw hawk

12 (5) (as above)

13 (5) *falcon god*

ḥr nḫn(y) (god) Horus of Nekhen

spdw (god) Soped

14 (5) ***nr, mt***

ʿḫmt riverbank

G - Birds (cont)

mwt mother, (goddess) Mut

mwt weight

msdmt, msḏmt kohl

mtn road

nrw terrible one

nrw terror

nrt vulture

nḫbt (goddess) Nekhbet

ssm(t) horse

sḏꜣmt pick

dwꜣ-mut a son of Horus

15 (5)

mwt (goddess) Mut

16 (5)

nbty The Two Ladies (king's title)

17 (2) *m, im*

m, im in, as, by, with, from, when, through, what

imy being of, who?, what?

im therein, there, thence

imy r overseer

in m wherewith?

m (negative imperative)

m n k take [to yourself] (imperative)

m behold

m who?, what?

mᶜ together with, in the hand of, from, owing to

mᶜ ntt seeing that

G - Birds (cont)

mwnf helper, companion

mfk3t, mfkt turquoise

mm among, therein, there, thence, wherewith

m h3w in the neighborhood of, at the time of

mhy be forgetful, negligent

mḫtbt an ornament

mk protect, behold!

r m to what end?

18 (5) *mm*

mm therein, there, thence, among, wherewith

mmy giraffe

tmm not having been

19 (5) *m, mi*

mhy be neglectful

20 (5) (as above)

21 (5) *nḥ*

nḥ guinea fowl

nḥi pray (for)

nḥb yoke together, unite

nḥbw yoked oxen

nḥb-k3w (a serpent deity)

nḥbt neck

nḥbt lotus bud

nḥp potter's wheel

nḥn rejoice

nḥḥ eternity, forever

G - Birds (cont)

 ***nḥsy*** Nubian

 ***nḥdt*** tooth

 ***nḥt*** prayer

 ***nt nḥḥ*** of eternity, for eternity

 ***tꜣ-nḥs(y)*** Nubia

22  (5) *ḏb*

 ***ḏbt*** brick

23  (5)

 ***rḫyt*** common people

24  (5) (as above)

 ***rḫyt*** common people

 ***dwꜣ rḫyt nb*** all the common people give praise

25  (5) *ꜣḫ*

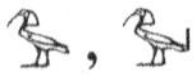 ***ꜣḫ*** spirit, spirit like nature

 ***ꜣḫ*** be glorious, beneficial, useful

 ***ꜣḫw*** power

 ***ꜣḫt*** what is good, useful, beneficial

 ***ꜣḫt*** arable land

 ***ꜣḫt*** flame

 ***ꜣḫt*** uraeus

 ***ꜣḫt*** god's eye, eye of Ra

 ***ꜣḫt*** horizon

 ***ꜣḫty*** of the horizon

 ***ꜣḫty*** of a remote people

 ***sꜣḫ*** glorify

 ***ꜣḫw*** glorifications, beatific spells

G - Birds (cont)

26 (5)

, ḏḥwty (god) Thoth

ḏḥwtt festival of Thoth

hb ibis

26 (5) (as above)

27 (5) *dšr* *flamingo, red*

dšr flamingo

dšr red

dšrt the Red Land, desert

28 (5) *gm*

ngmgm conspire

sgmḥ cause to see, glimpse

gmỉ find

gm wš found defective, destroyed

gmw mourning

gmḥ look at

gmḥsw hawk

gmḥt braided hair

gmḥt wick

gmgm break up, break

29 (5) *bꜣ*

ib(ꜣ) to dance

ibꜣr stallion

ꜥbꜣ aba sceptre

ꜥbꜣ stela, table of offerings

G - Birds (cont)

wbꜣ open up

wbꜣ open courtyard

bꜣ soul (in bird form)

bꜣ hack up, hoe (the earth)

bꜣ leopard skin

bꜣw boat

bꜣbꜣ hole, hiding place

bꜣbꜣt flowing stream

bꜣḥ foreskin, phallus

bꜣẖw outlying region east or west of Egypt

bꜣs jar

bꜣst Bubastis

bꜣstt (cat goddess) Ba

bꜣḳ fortunate

bꜣḳ oily

bꜣḳ moringa oil

bꜣḳ moringa tree

bꜣk servant

bꜣk work, task, decorated

bꜣkw work, task, decorated

bꜣkbꜣk a cake

bꜣkt work, task, labor, revenues, taxes

bꜣgi be remiss, slack, weary

bꜣgyw the dead

bꜣgsw dagger

bꜣt bush

bkꜣ tomorrow, morning

G - Birds (cont)

,  ***m bꜣḥ (ꜥ)*** in the presence of

, ,  ***nbꜣ*** pole

,  ***ẖbꜣ*** destroy, overwhelm

 ***ẖbwt*** (female) dancers

30  (5) ***bꜣw*** spirits, might

31  (5) *benu bird, heron*

,  ***bnw*** benu bird (pheonix)

 ***šnty*** heron

32  (5) *inundated*

, 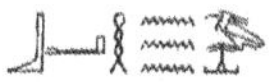 ***bꜥḥ*** be inundated, inundation, inundated land

,  ***bꜥḥi*** be inundated, inundate, have in abundance

,  ***bꜥḥ*** abundance

 ***bꜥḥ*** inundated land

33  (5) ***sdꜣ*** *tremble*

 ***sdꜣ*** egret bird

 ***sdꜣ*** tremble

 ***sdꜣdꜣ*** tremble

34  ,  ***niw*** ostrich

35  (5) ***ꜥḳ***

 ***ꜥḳ*** trusted one (who can enter freely)

 ***ꜥḳ(yw)*** intimates, friends

 ***ꜥḳyt*** female servant

 ***ꜥḳw*** provisions, revenue (in food), loaves

 [][] [ ***ꜥḳ [r][ḥr][m]*** enter [into][before][among]

G - Birds (cont)

36 (4) *wr*

imy wrt west side, starboard

w3d wr the sea

wr prince, great one, chief

wr how much?

wrỉ portion

wryt door posts

wr m3w "greatest of seers" (priestly title)

wr md administrative title

wrr great, important, much

wrr , wrt great, much, many, very

wrrt great crown

wrrt, wrryt, wryt chariot

wrḥ anoint, be anointed with

wrḥ ointment

wrs head rest, pillow

wrš spend all day, pass time

wršy watchman, sentry

wrt greatness

wrt the Great One (goddess)

wrt great crown

wrd , wrḏ to tire, be weary

mnt swallow

mr-wr Menevis bull

n-wr-n in as much as

ḫwrw wretch

G - Birds (cont)

swr promote, increase

swr to drink

swri drink

sḥwr vilify

37 (3) *small, narrow, bad, empty, perish, defective, ill*

ꜣyt pale, blanch (v)

ꜣꜥbt oppression

ꜣms lie, falsehood

ꜣhw pain, trouble, misery

ꜣhw sufferer

ꜣhmt sorrow

ꜣhd be feeble, faint

ꜣḳ perish

ꜣḳw ruin, misfortune

iyt mishap, harm

iw wrong, crime

iwyt wrongdoing ,

, ***(iw)t(y)(i)*** which not

ind illness, ill

iẖmt ignorant ones

, ***isft*** evil, wrongdoing, lie

isfty sinner

itmw lack of breath, suffocation

ꜥnd few

, ***wꜣsi*** be ruined, decay, ruin

wꜥꜥwt privacy

wn fault, failing, blame

G - Birds (cont)

wḫi escape, miss, fail

wḫt failure

wḫ3 be or act ignorant or foolish

, *wḫ3* fool, incompetent

wḫi escape, miss, fail

wsš die out

wšr dry up, be barren, be despoiled

, *wgg* misery, want, weakness

, *b3gi* be remiss, slack, weary

bin bad, miserable, act evilly

bgs bad, fractious

fn weak, infirm

fk be bald, bare

ft disgust, show dislike

mn ill, suffer, miserable

mr a sick man

mr ill, painful, sick, diseased

mr ib n be sorry for

mrḥ decay

mr ḥr ib n be displeasing to

mr a sick man

, *mrw* painfully

, *mrt* pains, disease

, , , *mḫy* be forgetful, negligent

nḫw loss, escape

msdi hate

nit wrong doing

G - Birds (cont)

nmḥ orphan

nhy little, few, some

nhw loss

nḏyt baseless

nḏs small, poor, feeble, dim

nḏs poor man, commoner, citizen, man

nḏsw poverty, low estate

hḳs deficient, stint, steal

ḥwrw wretch

ḥtm perish, be destroyed

ḥns be narrow

ḥḳr be hungry, hunger

ḥḳr hungry man

ẖbn be guilty, distorted

ẖbd to blame, disapprove of, be hateful

ẖnš stink

ẖsy weak, feeble, vile

ẖsyt wrongdoing

ẖks be injured

s‘nd to diminish

srẖ guilty one

sdḥ bring down, humiliate

šw empty

šrr be small, junior, short

ḳn offence

kt pettiness

g3w be narrow, constricted

G - Birds (cont)

gmw mourning

dḥi be low, lowly, hang down

dḥr bitter

dḥrt bitterness, sickness

ḏꜣyt transgression, wrong

38 (5) gb *bird, goose, idle, late* (see also **G39**)

ꜣpd bird, goose, duck, fowl

, ***idr*** flock of geese

wꜣꜣ talk, talk about, discuss

wsf be idle, idleness

wdf delay, lag, tardy

mnwt pigeon

niw ostrich

r a type of goose

, ***ḥb*** catch (of game)

, ***ḥtm*** perish, be destroyed

ḥtm perish

ḫt-ꜥꜣ poultry, edible fowl

sꜣty-gb "son of **Geb**"

***snḥm*(*w*)** locust(s)

šdw waterfowl

gb(b) the white fronted "**geb**" goose

gb (earth god) **Geb**

ṯrp a type of goose

ṯnḥr hawk

39 (5) sꜣ *pintail duck* (see also **G38**)

wsf be idle, idleness

G - Birds (cont)

pss results of labor

mswt young children or animals

ḥsꜣt sacred cow

sꜣ son

sꜣi linger, lag

sꜣw guard, protect, ward off, restrain

sꜣw beam, plank

sꜣ rꜥ son of Ra

sꜣty-bity the royal twins, Shu & Tefnet

sꜣty-gb "son of **Geb**"

sꜣtw ground, earth, floor

sꜥḳ cause to enter

sꜥḳ-nṯr god's entry

st, sꜣt pintail duck

40 (5) ***pꜣ, p*** (see also **G41**)

pꜣ the, this

pꜣ fly

pꜣy he of

pꜣy i my

pꜣ(w) have done

pꜣḳ flat cake, biscuit

pꜣt bread offering, loaf

pꜣwt primeval times, antiquity

pꜣwty primeval god

pꜣḏ a loaf

pss results of labor

spꜣ centipede

G - Birds (cont)

 ***spꜣt*** district, nome

41  (5) ***ẖn, ḳmi, sḥw, tn, ṯn*** (see also **G40**)

 ***ꜥẖi*** to fly, fly away

 ***wsf*** be idle, slack, sluggish, idleness

 ***wšꜣ*** fatten

,  ***pꜣ*** the, this

 ***pꜣy i*** my

 ***pꜣd, pd*** knee

 ***mtn, mṯn*** nomad hunter

 ***mṯn*** road

 ***rsf*** catch (of prey), affluence

 ***ḥtm*** perish, be destroyed

 ***ẖn*** rebel

 ***ẖn*** speech, sentence, utterance, matter, affair

 ***ẖni*** alight, halt

 ***ẖnw*** resting place, dwelling

 ***ẖnwt*** female musician

 ***ẖnt*** festival expense

 ***ẖpꜣ*** navel, umbilical

 ***ẖni*** alight, halt

 ***snm*** to feed (someone), feed on, eat, supply

 ***snm*** to be sad

 ***sḥwy*** collect, assemble

 ***sḥwy*** assemblage, collection

 ***sẖni*** alight

 ***sšꜣy [n]*** pray [to], supplication

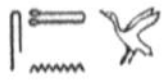 ***sṯny*** distinguish, honor

G - Birds (cont)

 ***ḳmꜣ*** throw

 ***ḳmꜣ*** create, nature, form

 ***ḳmyt*** gum, resin

 ***ṯni, ṯni*** to distinguish

 ***ṯnw*** number, each, every

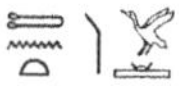 ***ṯnt*** difference

42  **(5)** *fat, provisions*

 ***wšꜣ*** fatten

 ***sḏfꜣy*** endow, provide for

 ***ḏf(ꜣ)w*** provisions

43  **(2) *w***

 ***wi*** I, me, my

 ***w*** one, someone

 ***w*** they, them, their

 ***w*** district, region

-  - ***w*** (verb suffix) which, who, -ing

-  -***w*** (plural suffix)

-  -***wt*** (fem. plural suffix)

-  -***wy*** (dual suffix) two, pair of, very, twice

 ***whi*** escape, miss, fail

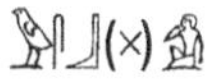 ***wšb*** answer

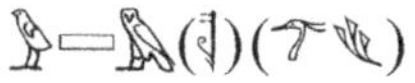 ***wšm*** ear (of corn)

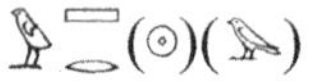 ***wšr*** dry up, be barren, be despoiled

 ***wtt, wtṯ*** beget

 ***wdi*** put, push, emit (a sound)

G - Birds (cont)

44 (5) *ww*

pḥww end

45 (5) *wꜥ*

wꜥw soldier

46 (5) *mꜣw*

m mꜣwt anew

47 (5) *ṯꜣ*

iṯꜣ thief

mṯꜣm sheer dress

mṯꜣt land inheritance

ṯꜣ nestling, young child

ṯꜣ pellet

ṯꜣi take, gird on, rob

ṯꜣ-ib able

ṯꜣy male, man

ṯꜣy bull calf

ṯꜣyw pellets

ṯꜣw breath, wind, air

ṯꜣw book

ṯꜣw take up, seize, rob

ṯꜣwt theft

ṯꜣwt sail

ṯꜣb a jar

ṯꜣbt loan (of grain)

ṯꜣm cloak, swaddling clothes

ṯꜣm be veiled

G - Birds (cont)

ṯ3m foreskin

ṯ3m ḥr m show indulgence to

ṯ3r fasten, make fast, preserve

ṯ3r cabin

ṯ3t(y) vizier

ṯnṯ3t canopy, dais

48 (5) *nest*

sšy nest

49 (5) *bird pool, nest, marsh*

sš marsh

sšy nest

50 (5) ***rḫty***

rḫty washerman

51 (5) *catch fish*

ḥ3m catch fish

52 (5) *feed*

snm feed (someone), feed on, eat

snmw food supply

53 (5)

b3 soul

54 (5) ***snḏ*** *associated with dead birds*

wšn wring the neck of, make an offering of

snḏ fear

snḏt fear

H - Parts of Birds

1  (5) *associated with dead birds*

 ***ꜣpd*** **(5)** goose, bird, fowl

 ***wšn*** wring the neck of, make an offering of

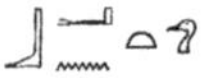 ***bꜥnt*** neck

2  (5) ***mꜣꜥ, wšm, pḳ***

 ***wšm*** ear (of corn)

 ***wšmw*** (beer) vessel

 ***pꜣḳt*** fine linen

 ***mꜣꜥ*** temple (of head)

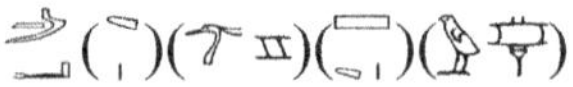 ***mꜣꜥ*** river bank

 ***mꜣꜥ*** real

 ***tp mꜣꜥ*** accompanying, escorting

3  (5) ***pꜣḳ, pḳ***

 ***pꜣḳ*** flat cake, biscuit

4  (5) ***nr***

 ***nr i*** to protect

 ***nrw*** terror

 ***rmṯ*** people, man, men, mankind

 ***snr*** take care of

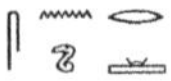 ***snr*** terrify

5  (5) *wing, fly*

 ***ꜥḫi, ꜥẖi*** to fly, fly away

 ***ꜥḫt*** to swoop

 ***pꜣ*** fly

 ***dmꜣt*** wing

 ***ḏnḥ, ḏnḥ*** wing

H - Parts of Birds (cont)

6  (5) ***šw***

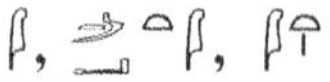 ***mꜣʿt*** truth, order

 ***mꜣʿt*** truth

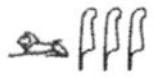 ***ršwt*** joy

 ***ḥm-nṯr-mꜣʿt*** prophet of Maat

 ***sšw*** to lose

 ***šw*** (air god) Shu

 ***šw*** be dry

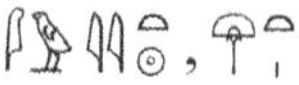 ***šwyt*** shadow, shade

 ***šww*** a herb, a gourd

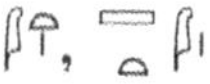 ***šwt*** feather

 ***šwt*** neighbors

6a  (5) (hieratic for words from the stem ***šw***)

7  (5) ***šꜣ***

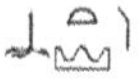 ***šꜣt*** (the land) Shat

8  (5) *female goddess, egg*

 ***ʿꜣt*** a valuable stone, stone vessel

 ***pꜣwty*** primeval god

 ***pʿt*** patricians, mankind

 ***sꜣ*** son

 ***swḥt*** egg

I - Amphibians, Reptiles, etc

1 (5) ***ꜥšꜣ*** *lizard*

ꜥšꜣ many, abundant, ordinary

ꜥšꜣ lizard

ꜥšꜣ dove

ꜥšꜣt multitude

ḥntꜣsw lizard

sꜥšꜣ multiply

2 (5) *turtle*

štyw turtle

3 (5) ***i͗t*** *greed, anger, voracious, crocodile*

ꜣd be aggressive, be angry, be savage, attack, anger

ꜣḏw aggressor

i͗ty sovereign

ꜥḫm voracious spirit

msḥ crocodile

ḥnt be greedy

ḫnty crocodile

sšd lightning flash

sšd gleam, glitter, flash

skn lust after

4 (5)

sbk (god) Sobek

5 (5) *collect, gather together*

sꜣḳ collect, gather together

5a (5)

sbk (god) Sobek

I - Amphibians, Reptiles, etc (cont)

6 (5) *km*

ikm shield

skm grey haired

kmy(t) herd (of cattle)

kmt Egypt

kmt a jar

7 (5) *Heket*

wḥm ꜥnḫ repeating life

ḥḳt (frog goddess) Heket

8 (5) *tadpole*

ḥfn, ḥfnw 100,000

ḥfnr tadpole

9 (2) *f* *father*

it father

f he, him, his, it, its

f3i carry, lift, weigh

f3i t3w sail

ft viper

mnfyt soldiers

P9 (5) *ḫr f*

ḫr(y).fy he says

S30 (5) *sf*

sf *yesterday*

U35 (5) *ḫsf*

ḫsf spin

I - Amphibians, Reptiles, etc (cont)

ḫsf repel, oppose

10 (2) *ḏ*

ỉp ḏt. f grow up (id) (lit - count his self)

mḏt deep, depth

mḏt stalled cattle

n ḏt. f his own

rḏd saying that

ḏf(ꜣ)w provisions

ḏs one's self, one's own

ḏt body, self

ḏt eternity, forever

ḏt estate, serf

ḏt serfs

ḏt cobra

ḏd say, speak, recite, think

ḏd mdw ỉn speech by, words spoken by

ḏd mdw speech (continued)

11 (5) *ḏd*

wḏdt what had been commanded

M14 (5) *wꜣḏ*

wꜣḏ fresh, be green, success, good fortune

wꜣḏ-wr the sea (lit. great green)

swꜣḏ hand over, bequeath

T5 (5) *ḥḏ* mace (see also **T3**)

ḥḏ white, be bright, light

ḥḏi damage

I - Amphibians, Reptiles, etc (cont)

T6 (5) *ḥḏḏ*

ḥḏḏwt brightness

V21 (5) *mḏ*

mḏ be deep

mḏt stable, cattle stall

12 (5) *goddess*

ꜣst (goddess) Isis

iꜥrt uraeus

wꜣḏyt (goddess) Wadjet

wrt the Great One (goddess)

nsrt (goddess) Nesret, uraeus, royal serpent

nt (goddess) **Neith**

nṯrt, ntrt goddess

rnnt nurse goddess

ḥnwt mistress

ḥḳt (frog goddess) Heket

sšmw divine shape, form, statue

sšmt guiding serpent

ḳrḥt local god, ancestral spirit

tfnt (goddess) Tefenet

13 (5) *goddess*

ꜣḫt uraeus

imt ḥꜣt f uraeus

wꜣḏyt (goddess) Wadjet

wꜥtt uraeus

nsrt (goddess) Nesret, uraeus, royal serpent

I - Amphibians, Reptiles, etc (cont)

nṯrt goddess

sʿryt uraeus

tpt uraeus

14 (5) *snake, serpent, worm*

ni͗k serpent demon

nʿw serpent

ḥfꜣw serpent

sbi͗ rebel serpent

ḏw the evil one

ḏdft snake

15 (5) (as above)

K - Fish

1 (5) ***in*** *catch (of game)*

in (a boat's) ropes

ini delay

inb(t) wall

inm skin

inḥ surround, enclose

inḥ eye brow(s)

inḳ envelop, embrace

int bolti fish

int valley

ind illness, ill

win reject, decline

wḥʿ fisherman, fowler

nm go wrong, steal

ḥb catch (of game)

sin delay, hasten, die

sinw ropes

sint clay seal

sint canoe

2 (5) ***bw***

bw hate, detest

bwytyw abominated ones

bwt abomination, detest

3 (5) ***ʿḏ, ʿd***

ʿdw buri fish

ʿḏ mr administrator (of a province)

K - Fish (cont)

4 (5) *ẖꜣ*

(i)ꜥbt ẖꜣt burial

mẖꜣ incline (to do)

ẖꜣyt pile of corpses

ẖꜣb sickle

ẖꜣb(t) curly appendage (on crown)

ẖꜣbb crookedness

ẖꜣmi bow down, bend over

ẖꜣmt ẖt pile of offerings

ẖꜣr sack, a large measure of capacity

ẖꜣrt widow

ẖꜣẖti tempest

ẖꜣkw-ib disaffected, rebel

ẖꜣt swamp, marsh

ẖꜣt oxyrhynchus fish

ẖꜣt quarry, mine

ẖꜣt corpse

5 (5) **bs** *fish, fishy smell*

bs, ibs [ḥr] introduce, enter [into], influx

bs mystery, mysterious form, secret

bsi flow, come forth in abundance

bsw secret image

mḥyt fish

nš supplant, drive away, expell

rm fish

rmw fish, fishy smell

ḫnš stink

K - Fish (cont)

6 (5) *fish scale*

, ***nšmt*** fish scale

6a (as above)

7 (5) *fish, discontent*

špt be discontented

81 (5)

nꜥr catfish

L - Invertebrates & Lesser Animals

1  (5) *ḫpr*

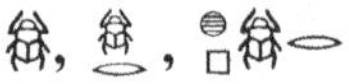 ***ḫpr*** come into existence, become, happen, make

 ***ḫprw*** form, shape, upbringing, stages of growth

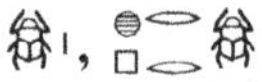 ***ḫprr*** dung beetle

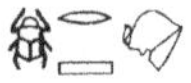 ***ḫprš*** the blue crown

 ***ḫprt*** occurrence

 ***ḫpr ḏs f*** he who created himself

2  (5) *bit*

 ***bit*** bee

 ***bit*** honey

 ***bity*** King of Lower Egypt

 ***pr-bity*** palace

 ***nsw bity*** King of Upper and Lower Egypt

 ***sꜣty-bity*** the royal twins, Shu & Tefnet

3  (5) *fly*

 ***ꜥff*** fly

3a  (5) (as above)

4  (5) *locust, grasshopper*

 ***snḥm*** locust, grasshopper

5  (5) *centipede*

 ***spꜣ*** centipede

6  (5) *ḫꜣ*

 ***ḫꜣt*** table of offerings

L - Invertebrates & Lesser Animals (cont)

7  (5)

 ***srḳt*** (goddess) Serket

81  (5) ***srḳ*** (O)

 ***srḳ*** scorpion

 ***srḳ*** breathe, inhale

M - Plants

1 (5) ***ỉ3m, ỉm*** *tree, fortune*

im(3), ỉ3m tree (general)

im3 be gracious, charming

im3t graciousness, charm, kindliness, favor

im(3)w splendor, brilliance

im(3)(w) tent

inhmn pomegranate

išd **"ished"** tree

isr tamarisk tree

ˁš cedar, pine, fir

b3ḳ moringa oil

b3ḳ moringa tree

bnrt date palm

mˁr be fortunate, successful

mnw trees, forest, plantation

nht sycamore-fig

nhwt trees

nbs a thorn tree

nḏm **"nedjem"** or carob tree

sim3 make well disposed

sbḳ leg, calf, splendid, precious

ssnḏm a type of wood or tree

šwb persea tree

ḳdtt a Syrian tree

ti šps a tree, a spice

ṯrt willow tree

1a (5) (as above)

M - Plants (cont)

2 (5) ***ḥn, is*** *plant, flower, light*

i reed

i3rw reeds

i3ḳt leeks

iḥwty tenant farmer

is be old

is chamber, tomb, workshop

isi be light

isy tomb, chamber

isw exchange, repay, reward

isw reeds

, ***iswt*** ancient times

idḥw Delta marshlands

ꜥr reed

ꜥrt sheet (papyrus or leather)

ꜥḥwty tenet farmer, field laborer

ꜥẖmw branches

w3ḥyt corn

wšm ear (of corn)

b3t bush

m3ḥ wreath

mnḥ papyrus plant

rnpwt vegetables, herbs

mḥ flax

ms bouquet

ḥn encumber, obstruct

ḥn control, occupy, commend

ḥn provide, equip, command, govern

M - Plants (cont)

ḥni rush

ḥnyt spear

ḥnw vessel

ḥnw (god) Sokar's bark

ḥnw commanders

ḥnwt horn

ḥnḥn be detain, hinder

ḥns be narrow

ḥnskt lock (of hair)

ḥnkw gifts

ḥnt occupation, craft

ḥnt two (both) sides (of)

ḥnty horse attendant

ḥrrt flower

ḥtpt bundle (of herbs)

ḫ3w plants

ḫrš bundle (of vegetables)

ḫdw onions

s man

smw pastures

sḥn decorate

sḥn to command

šww a herb, a gourd

dḥ3 straw

3 (3) **ḫt** *strong, wood, tree*

3ḫ3ḫ (ship's) spars

i3btt snare

iwsw balance, scale

M - Plants (cont)

ipdw furniture

imy ẖt who follows, accompanies, bodyguard, attendant, posterity

inb(t) wall

ispt quiver

ꜥꜣ column

ꜥꜣ door

ꜥwnt stick, club

ꜥfdt, ꜥfḏt chest, box

ꜥt room, chamber

ꜥḏ spool, reel

wrs head rest, pillow

wẖꜣ (wooden) column

wsr(w) oar

pds box

pdt bow, foreigners, troops

m ẖt after, afterward, accompanying

mstpt funeral bier

nꜥyt mooring post

nbꜣ pole

nẖt strong, victorious, victory, mighty

nẖtw strength, victories

nẖtt victory

r-ꜥ-ẖt combat, war

r ẖt under the authority of (lit- under the mast)

hbny ebony

ḥtꜥ bed

ẖꜥw funeral furniture, weapons, equipment

M - Plants (cont)

ẖt wood, timber, tree, woodland

ẖt tꜣw, ẖt mast

ẖt throughout, pervading, through

ẖti retire, retreat

ẖti retreat, be reversed

ẖti to carve, sculpture

ẖtyw threshing floor

ẖtyw terrace

ẖtwt furniture

ẖtẖt through

spw bundles of wood

ḳ(ꜣ)rt door bolt

ḳniw palanquin

gwꜣt

gsty palette

tmt sledge

tisw stick

ḏꜣ fire drill

ḏꜣḏꜣt harp

ḏbw pole (of chariot)

ḏrit wall

3a

(3)(see above)

ḏꜥr, ḏꜥ search out

4

(5) **rnp** *young, vigorous, time, year*

rnp colt

rnp young man

rnpi be young, vigorous

M - Plants (cont)

rnpt year

ḥꜣt-sp regnal year

ḥryw-rnpt epagomenal days

snf last year

tp-rnpt feast of the first of the year

tp-tr festival of the beginning of the season

tr time, season

tri show respect for

5 (5) *time, season*

pri battlefield

rnpw youthful vigor

tp-tr festival of the beginning of the season

tr time, season (see also below)

tꜣ-mri Egypt

6 (5) ***tr, ti, ri*** (see also above)

pri battlefield

ptr, pty who? what?

ptr behold, see

ḥtr team of horses, chariotry

ḥtr assess, tax, levy, provide

tr time, season (see also above)

tr pray

tri show respect for

tryt respect

7 (5) *young, vigorous*

rnpi be young, vigorous

M - Plants (cont)

rnpwt vegetables, herbs

ḥtr assess, tax, levy, provide

t3-mri Egypt

8 (5) *š3*

3ḫt inundation (season)

i3ḫ(i) be inundated

wš3 heap praises (on)

wš3 fatten

bš3 malted barley

š3 lotus pool, meadow

š3 appoint, command

š3yt fees, taxes

š3ᶜ begin, be first, spring, originate, beginning

š3ᶜ m beginning from

(r) š3ᶜ r as far as, down to

šwbty ushabti figure

š3bw food, meals

sš3y [n] pray [to], supplication

š3k bag

š3ty complement (of ship)

š3d to draw forth, rescue, educate, dig, dig out

š3w fate, destiny

9 (5) *lotus*

sšn, sššn lotus

sšn lotus shaped cup

M - Plants (cont)

10 (5) *lotus bud*

nḥbt lotus bud

11 (5) *offer, shore*

wdn offerer

wdn offer, make offerings, offering

wdnw offerings

w(ꜣ)ḏbw shores

12 (4) **ḫꜣ**

wḫꜣ (wooden) column

wḫꜣ hall of columns

wḫꜣ require, demand

wḫꜣ be or act ignorant or foolish

wḫꜣ fool, incompetent

mḫꜣ to balance, equal

pḫꜣ pavement

pḫꜣ split, break open, purge, clean, reveal

ḫꜣ 1,000

ḫꜣ administrative office

ḫꜣi measure

ḫꜣi examine

ḫꜣy plumb line

ḫꜣyt illness

ḫꜣyt slaughter, massacre

ḫꜣw bowl

ḫꜣw plants

ḫꜣw nw sšn lotus plants

M - Plants (cont)

ḫꜣwt (animal) hide

ḫꜣwt, ḫꜣy table of offerings

ḫꜣbt night, late evening

ḫꜣbb crookedness

ḫꜣfꜥ capture (in war)

ḫꜣmi bow down, bend over

ḫꜣmt ḫt pile of offerings

ḫꜣrw Khor (in Canaan)

ḫꜣrw one from Khor

ḫꜣrt widow

ḫꜣḫ hasten, swift, hurry, quick of speech, impatient

ḫꜣs scramble

ḫꜣst foreign land, hill country

ḫꜣt, ḫꜣwt, ḫꜣ(y)t table of offerings

ḫꜣt swamp, marsh

ḫꜣty office

ḫꜣtb have pity

ḫfꜥ seize, grip, grasp

ḫnrw reins

swḫꜣy decay

sḫꜣ remember

sḫꜣw remembrance, memory, memorial

13 (5) *wꜣḏ, w(ꜣ)ḏ*

wꜣḏ papyrus column

wꜣḏ papyrus

wꜣḏ a green stone

wꜣḏ success, good fortune

M - Plants (cont)

w3ḏ fortunate man

w3ḏ be green, fresh, vigorous, good fortune

w3ḏyt colonnade

w3ḏ wr the sea

w3ḏt cobra goddess

w3ḏt green linen

w3ḏt raw

wḏḥ weaned princeling

wḏ(t) to command, decree

swd renew, make green, make flourish, hand over, bequeath

14 (5) (see above)

w3ḏ success, good fortune, fresh, vigorous

w3ḏyt colonade

w3ḏ wr the sea (lit - the great green)

w3ḏt green linen

15 (5) **w3ẖ, 3ẖ** *watery regions, papyrus*

i3ẖi be inundated

iẖi to make flourish

idḥy Delta marsh man

idḥw Delta marshlands

3ẖ papyrus thicket

3ẖ-bit N. Delta town of Chemmis

w3ẖy palace reception hall, columned

mḥw papyrus clump

mḥ-s crown of Lower Egypt

mḥt Delta marshes

t3-mḥw Lower Egypt, the Delta

M - Plants (cont)

 ***ḏyt*** papyrus marsh

 ***ḏt*** papyrus stem

16  (5) *ḥꜣ*

 ***is-ḥꜣḳ*** plunder

 ***wḥꜣ*** pull up (a plant), hew (stone)

 ***wḥꜣt*** cauldron

 ***wḥꜣt*, *wḥt*** oasis

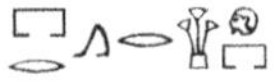 ***pr r ḥꜣ*** go forth abroad

 ***mḥ-s*** crown of Lower Egypt

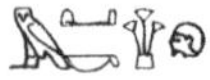 ***mkḥꜣ*** to neglect

 ***nbwt*** aegean islands

 ***nḥꜣ*** shake

 ***nḥꜣ*** be hard, rough, dangerous, contrary, perverse

 ***ḥꜣ*** would that!

 ***ḥꜣ*** outside

 ***ḥꜣ*** back of head, behind, around

 ***ḥꜣyw*** carrion-birds

,  ***ḥꜣʿyt*** strife, discontent

 ***ḥꜣwy*** naked man

 ***ḥꜣw-mr*** the lower orders

 ***ḥꜣw-ḫt*** special offering

 ***ḥꜣp*** secret place

, ,  ***ḥꜣp*** conceal, hide, secret mysterious

 ***ḥꜣḳ(t)*** plunder, capture, carry off

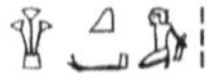 ***ḥꜣḳw*** captives

 ***ḥꜣd*** fish trap, trap fish

 ***tꜣ-mḥw*** Lower Egypt, the Delta

M - Plants (cont)

dḥ3 straw

17 (2) *i*

i reed

i say

i "O"

i I, me, my

i3w to praise

iˁ3, i3ˁ skirt

iw indeed, verily, in fact, it happed that, (etc) (a part of the verb "to be" but implies fact, difficult to translate and is sometimes omitted)

ibwy halyards (of boat)

ip to count, calculate, reckon, access, pay, examine, heed, assemble

ipw, iptw that

ipn, iptn this

ipt reckoning, census

ip ḏt. f grow up (id) (lit - count his self)

ifdt four of, quartet

im there, therein, therewith

im in, as, by, with, from, together with

imy mine, yours

imy being in

imn (god) Amun

in to, for, of, through, in, by (agent), because, not (etc)

in indeed

in says

in m wherewith?

ir as for, as to, if

ir to, at, concerning, from, more than, so that, until, according as

M - Plants (cont)

 ,  ***iry, irw*** from, thereof, thereto, make

 ***irf*** (gives emphasis to a command or question)

 ***irt*** (used for emphasis with "you")

 ***ir ṯn*** (used for emphasis with "you")

 ***iḫw*** a measure of metal

 ***iḫt*** thing(s)

 ***is*** indeed

 ***ispr*** whip

 ***ispt*** throne

 ***isk*** Lo!

,  ***isṯ, ist*** Lo!, behold, now

 ***isfty*** sinner

 ***išdd*** sweat

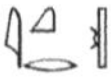 ***iḳr*** excellent, precious, virtue, trustworthy

 ***it*** father

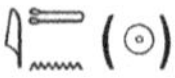 ***itn*** (god) Aten

 ***idn*** lay out

17a  **(2)** ***y***

 ***y*** (*suffix meaning* being or having)

18  **(5)** ***i***

 ***ii*** come, Welcome!

 ***ii-wy*** how welcome (is), Welcome!

 ***iyt*** mishap, harm

19  **(5)** *offering, desirable*

 ***ꜥ3b*** pleasant, pleasing, desirable

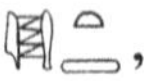,  ***ꜥ3bt*** offering, pile of offerings

M - Plants (cont)

20  (5) ***sm, sḫt***

 ***sm*** occupation, pastime

, ,  ***sḫt*** marshland, country

 ***sḫt*** the marsh goddess

 ***sḫty*** peasant

 ***sḫtyw*** class of cattle

21  (5) ***sm***

,  ***sm*** herb, plant

 ***sm*** succour

22  (5) ***nḫb***

, ,  ***nḫb*** Nekheb (El Kab) (UE)

 ***nḫbt*** germination, shooting up

, 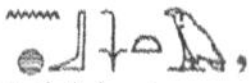, , , ,  ***nḫbt*** (goddess) Nekhbet

22a  (5) ***nn***

, 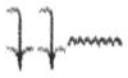 ***nn*** this, these

 ***nn(i)*** be weary

 ***nnt*** rushes

 ***rnn*** caress

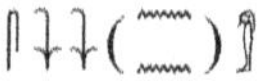 ***snn*** image, portrait

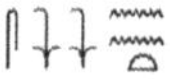 ***snnt*** likeness

23  (5) ***sw*** (see also **M24** and **M26**)

 ***iwsw*** balance, scale

 ***b3gsw*** dagger

 ***pr-nsw*** palace

 ***m3gsw*** dagger

 ***ny-sw*** he belongs to

M - Plants (cont)

nsy be king

nsyw kings

nsyt kingship

nsw King

nsw bity King of Upper and Lower Egypt

nsw ẖkryt king's ornament (concubine title)

ḫnsw the tenth month, (moon god) Khonsu

sw he, him, it, his, its

swt sedge plant

swt but, he, it, she

tisw stick, staff

24 (5) *rsw*

rsy south, southern

rsw southerners

rsw south wind

rswt south

25 (5) (faulty writing for **M24** or **M26**)

rs(y)w southerners

rswt south land

smʿ Upper Egyptian corn

26 (5) *šmʿ*

it Upper Egyptian barley, corn

šmʿ barley from Upper Egypt

šmʿ make music

šmʿyt chantress

šmʿ(w) Upper Egypt)

šmʿw iwnw (Heliopolis of UE) Thebes (UE)

M - Plants (cont)

27 (5) ***šmꜥ*** (see also **M26**)

šm make music

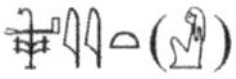

šmꜥyt chantress

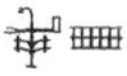

šmꜥ(w) Upper Egypt

28 (5) (see also **M26**)

wr md (administrative title) "Greatest of the tens of Upper Egypt"

29 (5) ***nḏm***

mnfrt (arm) band

nmꜥ [n] show partiality [to], question

nḏm "**nedjem**" or carob tree

nḏm sweet, agreeable, pleasant, well, comfortable

nḏm ib joyful

snḏm make happy, ease

snḏm sit

ssnḏm a type of wood or tree

30 (5) *sweet, date*

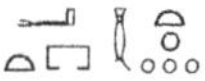

ꜥt bnrt date-cake room

bnr dates

bnrt date palm

bnrt sweetness

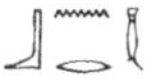

bnri sweet

31 (5) ***rd*** *grow*

rwdw agent

rd to grow

M - Plants (cont)

32 (5) (as above)

r(w)d be strong

srd to grow, to erect

33 (5) *grain, corn*

, , ***it*** barley, corn

mḥ Lower Egyptian corn

npri (grain god) Nepri

šmʿ Upper Egyptian corn

bty emmer wheat

34 (5)

, ***bdt, bty*** emmer wheat

šf-tbt the sixth month

35 (5) *heaps*

ʿḥʿ heap, proportion, allotment

ʿḥʿw heaps

wbn overflow

nb ʿḥʿw wealthy man (lit - lord of heaps)

ẖtyw threshing floor

36 (5) ***ḏr*** *bind*

msḏr ear

mḏr shut out

nḏri to hold fast, catch, arrest, obey, follow, take possession of

nḏrt imprisonment

r-ḏr-f entire

sḏr lie, spend the night, sleeping

sḏr lie prostrate

sḏr department

M - Plants (cont)

sḏryt slaughter

ḏmꜣ bind together

ḏr since, end

ḏr, ḏri wall

ḏri hard, firm, stoutly

ḏrit wall

ḏr ꜥ(wy) originally, long ago, end, limit

ḏr ꜥ r down until

ḏrw boundary, limit

ḏrw side

ḏrwy color, paint

ḏrwt hall

ḏr bꜣḥ formerly

ḏr ntt since, because

ḏrt hand, recite

ḏrtyw ancestors

ḏrḏ tree leaf

ḏrḏri foreigner, foreign

37 (5) *ḏr* (as above)

38 (5) *flax, bind*

mḥꜥ flax

ḏmꜣ bind together, cut off (heads)

39 (5) *vegetable offerings*

rnpwt vegetables, herbs

ḥnkt offerings

40 (5) ***is***

imy is councilor

M - Plants (cont)

is chamber, tomb, workshop

is be old

isi be light (weight)

isw reeds

iswt ancient times

iswt gang, crew

isft evil, wrongdoing, lie

isfty sinner

ist palace

41 (5) *wood*

ꜥš cedar, pine, fir

wꜥn juniper

mr(w) Syrian red "**meru**" wood

42 (5) *wn* (see also **E34**)

wnm eat

wn-mꜣꜥ truth, reality

wnm(w)t food

wnm eat

wnn exist, be

wn-nfr Osiris

wnḏw short horned cattle

wnḏwt subjects, people, associates

ḥwn youthful, youth, vigor, be young, refreshed, child, young man

ḥwnt maiden

sswn destroy, destruction

M - Plants (cont)

43 (5) *vine, gardener, fruit*

i͗ꜣrrt vine

i͗ꜣrrt grapes

i͗rp wine

i͗šd fruit of the "**ished**" tree

ꜥꜣb pleasant, pleasing, desirable

ꜥꜣbt self-seeking, selfishness

ꜥꜣbt food provisions

šꜣbw food, meals

kꜣmw vintner

kꜣnw garden

kꜣny, kꜣry gardener, vintner

dꜣbw figs

44 (5) *sharp, thorn*

prt rising of Sothis

spd sharp

spdw (god) Soped

srt thorn

sspd make ready, supply

t ḥḏ white bread

83 (5) ***sšn*** lotus plant

84 (5) ***smꜣ*** union of Upper and Lower Egypt

85 (5) ***r*** (same use as **D21,**) (L)

N - Sky, Earth, Water

1 (5) ***ḥry, ḥrw*** *high, above, sky, heaven*

in-ḥrt (god) Onuris

idw pestilence

ꜥḫi hang up

wbꜣ open courtyard

biꜣ firmament

pt sky, heaven

nwt (goddess) Nut

rwty outside

r-ḥry master, chief

ḥꜣt ceiling

ḥꜣyt portal

ḥry above, who is over, captain

ḥry captain, chief, who is over, upper

ḥry pḏt troop commander

ḥry-ḫt-f offering loaf

ḥrt-š garden

ḥry-tꜣ survivor

ḥry-tp chief, chieftain, who is upon, who is over

ḥrw upper part, top

ḥrt hill-side tomb

ḥrt sky, heaven

ḫi hang

smsw hyt elder of the portal

sḥr fly aloft

gs-ḥry top, uppermost

N - Sky, Earth, Water (cont)

1a (5)

tpḥt cavern, snake hole

2 (5) *darkness, dusk, night*

ꜥḫḫw dusk, twilight

wḫ night, dark

wḫt darkness

msyt supper, evening meal

mšrw evening

hꜣwy night, late evening

knḥ dark

kk be dark

kkw darkness

grḥ night

ḏꜣw night

3 (5) (as above)

4 (5) *rain, dew*

idw pestilence

iꜣdt dew, pouring rain

idt fragrance

ḫꜣḫti tempest

šni put down (strife)

šnyt rain storm

5 (5) *time, sun, day*

ꜣbd month

ꜣt instant, moment

ꜣt striking power, attack

N - Sky, Earth, Water (cont)

im(ꜣ)w splendor, brilliance

iṯn, itn (god) Aten

ꜥḥꜥw period (of time), lifetime

ꜥrḳy last day (of month)

wbn shine, (sun) rise

wbnw eastern

wnwt hour, priestly duties

wrš spend all day, pass time

wršy watchman, sentry

wšr dry up, be barren, be despoiled

prt winter season

psd, psḏ shine

psḏntyw, psdn, psḏn New moon festival

mꜣ-ḥsꜣ lion

min today

(m) mnt daily

nw time

nhp rise early

nhpw early morning

nḥḥ eternity, forever

nt nḥḥ of (for) eternity

rꜥ (god) Ra, sun

rꜥ (god) Ra

rꜥ nb every day

rꜥt sun goddess (said of queen)

ršršt rejoice

rk time, period

hrw day

N - Sky, Earth, Water (cont)

ḥb sd "Sed" festival, jubilee

ḥḏ white, be bright

sw day (in dates)

sf yesterday

snkt darkness

sšp daylight

šw sun, be dry

šwyt shadow, shade

šmw summer

šmw harvest

kꜣ-ḥr-kꜣ fifth month festival

tp-iꜣt due time (to act)

tp-rꜥ-mḏ 10 day week

tp-tr festival of the beginning of the season

tr time, season

dwꜣw morning, tomorrow, rise early, dawn

dwꜣt, dwꜣyt morning

dmḏyt festival cycle

dnit a festival

6 (5)

rꜥ (god) Ra, sun

7 (5)

ḫrt-hrw daytime

8 (5) *wbn, ḥnmmt* *sunshine*

ꜣḫw sunshine

im(ꜣ)w splendor, brilliance

iḫḫw dusk

N - Sky, Earth, Water (cont)

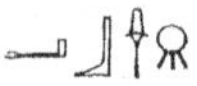 ***ꜥb(ꜣ)*** shine, glitter

 ***wbn*** shine forth, rise (sun)

 ***wbnw*** wound

 ***wgb*** rise

 ***psd, psḏ*** shine

 ***mꜣwt*** rays (of light)

 ***ḫnmmt*** sun people of Heliopolis

 ***ḥḏ*** white, be bright

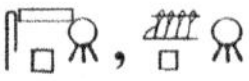 ***šsp, sšp*** daylight

 ***stwt*** rays

 ***šw ɨ*** be dry

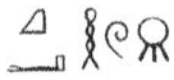 ***ḳꜥḥw*** sunrise

9  (5) ***psḏ***

 ***psḏntyw, psḏn*** New moon festival

 ***psḏt*** ennead, the nine gods

 ***pgꜣ*** unfold, spread out, reveal

10  (5) (as above)

11  (5) *moon, mouth, palm*

 ***ꜣbd*** month

 ***iꜥḥ*** moon

 ***wꜥḥ*** carob beans

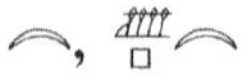 ***šsp*** palm (measure)

 ***dwꜣ*** adore

12  (5) (as above)

13  (5)

 ***nt*** half month festival

N - Sky, Earth, Water (cont)

14 𓇼 (5) *sbꜣ, dwꜣ* *constellation, star*

ỉẖm sk indestructible

ꜣbd month

wnwt hour, priestly duties

wnwt priesthood

wnwt(y) hour watcher, astrologer

bkꜣ tomorrow, morning

prt rising of Sothis

msẖtyw Great Bear constellation

ẖpš Great Bear constellation

sꜣḥ (constellation) Orion

sbꜣ star

sbꜣ teach

sbꜣ door, entrance

sbꜣyt teachings, instructions

spdt (star) Sothis (Sirius)

sšd lightning flash

gnẖ serve

gnẖt star

dwꜣ adore, praise

dwꜣw morning, tomorrow, rise early, dawn

dwꜣ-mut a son of Horus

dwꜣt adore, praise

dwꜣt, dwꜣyt morning

dwꜣt netherworld

15 𓇽 (5)

d(w)ꜣt netherworld

N - Sky, Earth, Water (cont)

16 (5) *tꜣ* *earth, land, estate, eternity, serf*

wpt tꜣ earth's beginning, the extreme south

pr-ḏt estate

rdỉ r tꜣ to land, throw down, neglect

ḥry-tꜣ survivor

ḫntyw-tꜣ Southerners

sštꜣ mystery, secret

, , *tꜣ* land, earth

tꜣwy the two lands, Egypt

, *tꜣ-wr* larboard, west bank

() *tꜣ-mrỉ* Egypt

tꜣ-nḥs(y) Nubia

tꜣ ḏsr necropolis

tpyw tꜣ the living

tp(y)-tꜣ survivor

dhn tꜣ touch forehead to ground

ḏt eternity, forever

, *ḏt* estate, serf

ḏt serfs

17 (5) *tꜣ* (same as **N16**)

18 (5) *ỉ* *desert, foreign land* (see also **N16, S26, X4** and **Z8**)

, *ꜣḫt* horizon

ỉw island

ỉrt Yareth (in Syria)

ỉsft evil, wrongdoing, lie

, *w* island

bꜣḥ a measure of capacity

N - Sky, Earth, Water (cont)

,  ***p3wt*** primeval times, antiquity

 ***stt*** Asia, Sehel Island (by Aswan, UE)

, 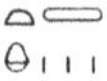 ***t*** bread

, ,  ***t3-tmw*** all men

, ,  ***ṯḥnw*** Libya

,  ***ṯḥnt*** faience, glass

19  **(5)** *desert, foreign land*

,  ***3ḫty*** of the horizon

 ***ḥr-3ḫty*** Horus of the horizon, Horakhti

20  **(5) *wḏb*** *shore*

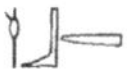 ***wḏb*** sand bank, shore

 ***wḏb*** turn back

 ***psn*** a loaf

, ,  ***ḥb sd*** "**Sed**" festival, jubilee

 ***spt*** side edge of a boat

 ***sd*** jubilee

21  **(4)** *bank, land, field, town* (see also **N23**)

,  ***3ḥt*** field, arable land, earth

 ***i3btyw*** the east of

 ***iwtn*** ground, floor

 ***ꜥḫmt*** river bank

 ***ist*** mound

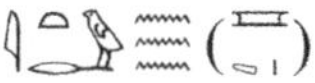 ***itrw*** river, Nile

 ***itrw*** length of 6.5 mi

, ,  ***idb*** bank, region

 ***idbwy*** the two banks, Egypt

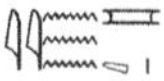 ***ym*** sea

N - Sky, Earth, Water (cont)

w3ḏ wr the sea (lit. - great green)

wḏb sandbank, shore, river bank

bi3 firmament, heaven

pri battlefield

pḥww marshlands, far north, distant marshlands, outer limits, ends of the earth

pḥww m northward to

pg3 opening, mouth, entrance

pdswt Delta dunes

m3ʿ river bank

nmw vats

nḫb fresh land

rs(y)w southerners

rswt south

ḥbbt water

ḥrt-š garden

ḫ3s creek

ḫbsw cultivated lands

ḫntyw tenants

ḫntyw-t3 Southerners

ḫnt š wooded country, garden

s3ḥ grant, endowment (of land)

s3tw ground, earth, floor

sbty surrounding wall, rampart

spt shore

smdt subjects, subordinates, staff

sš marsh

šd artificial lake

N - Sky, Earth, Water (cont)

sḏ break into, invade

šdy ditch

šdyt rubble

šdw plot of ground

tꜣ land, earth

, , *tꜣš* boundary

tꜣ-tmw all men

ṯs-pri fighting

ṯst ridge, range

, *dꜣiw* loin cloth

dmi town

22 (5) *land, field*

ꜥḥt field

23 (4) *irrigated land, boundary, (rarely) time* (see also **N21**)

ꜣꜣ ruin(s)

, *ꜣḥt* field, arable land, earth

ꜣḫt arable land

, *iḫmt, ꜥḫmt* river bank

itrw river, Nile

idḥw Delta marshlands

ꜥmꜥ smear mud

, , , *ꜥḏ, ꜥd* desert edge, limit of cultivation

w island

w district, region

pḫr wr Euphrates River

pgꜣ opening, mouth, entrance

()()()() *mꜣꜥ* river bank

N - Sky, Earth, Water (cont)

mʿḥʿt, miḥʿt tomb

nẖb fresh land

ndbwt area, full extent

rk time

ḥry-tꜣ survivor

ẖbsw cultivated lands

ẖrw low lying land

ẖrp district, estate

ẖtyw threshing floor

ẖꜣt, ẖꜣt swamp, marsh

sꜣtw ground, earth, floor

sntt ground plan, foundation

skꜣt cultivated land

sš marsh

šdyt pool, plot of land

šdw, šdwt plot of ground

tꜣ land

tꜣ-wr larboard, west bank

tꜣš boundary, frontier

tr time, season

ṯs sandbank

24 (5) *district, nome, garden*

ḥsp garden

šmʿw Upper Egypt

spꜣt district, nome

ḳn mat

ḏꜣtt estate

N - Sky, Earth, Water (cont)

25  (5) *foreign land, hill country, desert*

 ***ꜣbw*** Elephantine (UE)

 ***iꜣbt*** east

 ***iꜣbtyw*** the east of

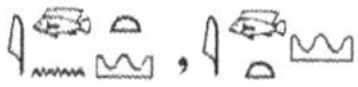 ***int*** valley

 ***i(w)grt*** necropolis

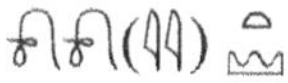 ***wꜣwꜣt*** Northern Nubia, Kush

 ***wꜣwt*** Roads of Horus

 ***wḥꜣt*, *wḥt*** oasis

 ***wdrt*** region

 ***bꜣẖw*** outlying region east or west of Egypt

 ***biꜣw*** mine

 ***biꜣt*** quarry

 ***pwnt*** Punt (Somalia)

 ***mrw*** desert

 ***msḳt*** the Milky Way

 ***mḏꜣw*** Medja in Nubia

 ***nhrn, nhꜣrynꜣ*** Naharin (Eastern Mesopotamia, between the Tigris and Euphrates rivers)

 ***r ꜣw*** Turah (limestone quarry site)

 ***rmnn*** Lebanon

 ***r-stꜣw*** necropolis (of god Sokar)

 ***rṯnw*** Retjnu (Syria)

 ***ḥꜣ*** (god) Ha

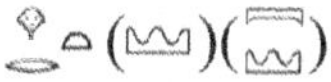 ***ḥrt*** hill-side tomb

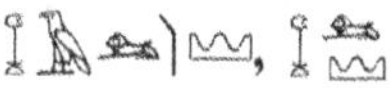 ***ḫꜣrw*** Khor (in Canaan)

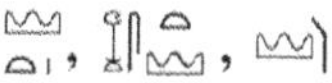 ***ḫꜣst*** foreign land, hill country

 ***ḫꜣstyw*** foreigners, desert dwellers

N - Sky, Earth, Water (cont)

ḫnt-ḥn-nfr Nubian region south of the second cataract

ḫt Hatti, land of the Hittite

smt desert, necropolis

sṯt, stt Asia, Sehel Island (by Aswan, UE)

styw Nubians

š3rḥ3n Sharahan (border town between Egypt and Syro-Palestine)

šm(3)w wanderers, strangers, foreigners

kpn(y) Byblus (in Phoenicia)

knmtyw those who dwell in darkness

kš Kush (Nubia, the area south of the first cataract at Aswan)

t3-mri̓ Egypt

t3-nḥs(y) Nubia

t3 ḏsr necropolis

tmḥi̓ Temhi land

ṯḥnt faience, glass

ṯst ridge, range

dšrt the Red Land, desert

ḏ3hy part of Phoenicia and Canaan

26 (5) *ḏw, dw*

3bḏw Abydos (UE)

wnḏw short horned cattle

wnḏwt subjects, people, associates

rḏw efflux

sḏwy slander

ḏw mountain

dw be bad, evil, sad

ḏw the evil one

N - Sky, Earth, Water (cont)

ḏwi call

ḏws malign

ḏwt evil, sadness

ḏww mountains

27 (5) ***ȝḫt***

ȝḫt horizon

ȝḫt horizon, tomb

ȝḫty of the horizon (dweller)

28 (5) ***ḫʿ***

ḫʿ hill of the sunrise

ḫʿi appear, shine

ḫʿw crown

ḫʿw funeral furniture, weapons, equipment

ḫʿw weapons

ḫʿw-nw--r-ʿ-ḫt weapons of war

ḫʿm approach, appear

ḫʿr to rage

29 (2) ***ḳ***

ḳȝȝ hill, height

ḳȝbw winding (of river)

ḳȝs to bind, string

ḳnn superiority

30 (5)

ist mound

31 (5) *road, travel ,distance, position*

iʿr, ʿr ascend, mount, approach

N - Sky, Earth, Water (cont)

ꜥrw neighborhood

ỉn-ḥrt (god) Onuris

ꜥꜣ here, there, yonder

swꜣ pass by, escape, surpass, pass away, remove, transgress, occur

ꜥr ascend, mount up, approach

wꜣ far, distant, long

wꜣwt Roads of Horus

wꜣr fall into (a bad state)

wꜣt road, way, side

wp-wꜣwt (the wolf god) Wepwawet

pf that, yonder

mṯn road

r wꜣt path, passage

r ssy entirely, quite, at all

ḥnty period

ḥr (falcon god) Horus

ḥr [r] be far, distant [from]

ḥrw-(r) apart from, as well as, besides

ḥrt road

sꜥr make to ascend, offer up

sꜥryt uraeus

sḥrỉ drive away, banish

tp-wꜣt journey, beginning (of reign)

ḏrw boundary, limit

32 (5) ***sinw*** *clay, dirt* (see also **Aa2** and **F52**)

mḥsḥs filthy one

sinw runners

33 ○ (3) *sand, metal, mineral, pellet, medicine*

iꜣrrt grapes

wꜥḥ carob beans

bꜣbꜣ hole, hiding place

pẖrt medicine, prescription

pꜣḳ flat cake, biscuit

mnḥ wax

msdmt black eye paint, kohl

nhy little, few, some

ḥmꜣt salt

ẖnmt red jasper, carnelian

spw fragments

spw bundles of wood

smꜣt-ꜥ an offering

sntr incense

šꜥy sand

ḳd build, fashion (pots)

gy an offering loaf

ṯꜣ pellet

ṯswrt offering loaf

dnit bowl

ḏrwy color

ḏꜥbt charcoal

33a ○○○ (3) (as above, but plural)

ꜣs soft inner body parts

ꜥprw jewelry

ꜥgt varnish

N - Sky, Earth, Water (cont)

ꜥt bnrt date-cake room

wꜥꜥwt privacy

wṯtw offspring

wꜣḏ a green stone

wꜥḥ carob beans

bnr dates

pꜣwt primeval times, antiquity

mfkꜣt turquoise

mḥtyw northerners

mtr fame, renown

msdmt, msḏmt kohl

nbw gold

nbwt Aegean islands

ndbwt area, full extent

ḥmꜣgt carnelian

ḥnkt offerings

ḥsmn bronze

ḫftyw enemies

ḫsbd lapis lazuli

ẖkrw ornament, insignia

sꜣwy 2/3 fine gold

snṯr, sntr incense

sḫtyw class of cattle

styw Nubians

šꜥt slaughter, ferocity, blood lust

špssw riches, wealth

šsrw bags

ḳmyt gum, resin

N - Sky, Earth, Water (cont)

gnwt annals

ṯȝyw pellets

dnwt families

dḥty lead

dḳ flour, powder

dḳr(w) fruit

33b **(3)** (as above)

34 **(5)** *copper or bronze objects, weapons*

ꜥnḫ mirror

whȝt*, *wḥt cauldron

bȝgsw dagger

mȝgsw dagger

minb axe

mss corselet

mšw sword

ḥmt, biȝ copper

ḥsmn bronze

ḫꜥw weapons

sswt metal inlay

šfdw a ritual object

ḳrdn axe

dbn helmet

35 **(2)** ***n***

n we, us, our

n, in to, for, of, through, in, because, not (etc)

-n (past tense - suffix)

n, nn not

N - Sky, Earth, Water (cont)

nꜣ this, these

nis invoke, summon, recite

ny, mw, n therefor, for

ny them

nbyt beaded collar

nf that

n m, in m who, what

nnk mine, on my part

nhw protection

nhw loss, escape

nẖ to defend, protect, protection

nss do damage

ngsgs overflow

nt water

nty who, which

nty who, which

ntʿ custom, observances

ntf he, his

ntf, nty f which he

nts she

ntsn they

ntk you, yours

ntk, ntyk which you

ntt that

ntṯ, ntt you

ntṯn, nttn you

nḏt subjects, serfs

N - Sky, Earth, Water (cont)

35a (5) ***mw*** *water, liquid, wash, drink, river, lake*

iꜥi wash, cleanse

iꜥi ib satisfy (one's) wrath, appetite, desire

iwḥ to moisten, water, irrigate

ibḥ priest who performs libations

ibḥw one who performs libations

itrw river, Nile

itrw length of 6.5 mi

ym sea

ynꜥm Yenoam (in Palestine)

ꜥ dyke

ꜥḫm quench, extinguish, destroy

wꜣw wave

wꜣḏ wr the sea (lit. - great green)

wꜥb be pure, clean

wꜥbt tomb, sanctuary, embalming place

wḏnw torrent, flood

bꜣbꜣt, bbt flowing stream

bꜥbꜥ drink

bꜥbꜥt stream

bꜥḥ be inundated, inundation, inundated land abundance

bꜥḥ abundance

bgꜣw shipwrecked man

pḥww marshlands

fdt sweat

mi(w) waters

myw sperm

N - Sky, Earth, Water (cont)

mw water

mwy urine, semen, saliva

mww muu dancers

mw-pf-ḳdw the Euphrates River

mḥi drown, launch (a boat)

mḥyt north wind

mḏt deep, depth

nwy(t) water, flood

nwyt waters of a river, canal, etc.

nbi to swim

ntf to water, irrigate, sprinkle

r-ḥꜣt mouth (of river)

hdmw footstool

ḥwi surge up, overflow, rain

ḥwyt rain

ḥbbt water

ḥr mw n loyal to (lit - on the water of)

ẖnw brook, stream

ẖnmt well, cistern, water source

siwḥ rob

siwḥ inundate

swꜥb purify, cleanse

swri drink

šmw summer

šmw harvest

ḳbḥw sky

tyntꜥ Tineta (water channel in Nubia)

ṯhi drink deep

N - Sky, Earth, Water (cont)

ḏdkw channel, canal

36 (5) ***mr, mi͗*** *river, lake, sea, inundation, channel*

i͗trw river, Nile

i͗trw length of 6.5 mi

ꜥḏ mr administrator (of a province)

ym sea

wꜣḏ wr the sea (lit. - great green)

pnꜥyt cataract

pḥww marshlands, far north, distant marshlands, outer limits, ends of the earth

pẖr wr Euphrates River

mi͗nb axe

mi͗ḥꜥt tomb

mi͗st liver

mr canal, channel, libation trough

mr friends, partisans

mri͗ love

mrw overseer of weavers

mrt weavers, servants, underlings

mẖr low-lands

nwy water, flood

nmw vats

r-ḥꜣt mouth (of river)

ḥꜣw-mr the lower classes

ḥꜥpy, ḥp the inundation

ẖnw stream, brook

ẖnmt well, cistern, water source

ḏdkw channel, can

N - Sky, Earth, Water (cont)

37 (2) *š* *water source, irrigated land* (see also **X4**)

w3ḏ wr the sea (lit. - great green)

ḥʿpyw inundations

, *ẖnmt* well, cistern, water source

sṯ3t aroura (land measure)

š pool

() *šfšft* ram's head, respect, awe

št3t secrets

štyw an offering loaf

šd artificial lake

38 (5)

sṯ3t aroura (also as above)

U18 (5) *grg*

, , *grg* found, establish, snare

, , *grg* lie, falsehood

39 (5) (see **N37** above)

40 (5) *šm*

, *šm* go

41 (5) *ḥm, bi3* *well, pool, marsh, female organ*

ʿḥʿ ḥmsi pass one's life

iry ḥmw helmsman

iri hmt take a wife

() *iḥms* occupant (in titles), attendant

iḥms sit down, dwell, besiege

iḥmst session of king and courtiers

iḥ ḥmt cow

N - Sky, Earth, Water (cont)

 ***idt*** cow

 ***idt*** vulva, womb

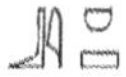 ***biꜣ*** copper

 ***biꜣ*** firmament, heaven

 ***biꜣ*** firmament

 ***biꜣy*** made of bronze

 ***biꜣw*** mine

 ***biꜣyt*** wonder, marvel

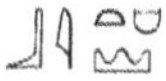 ***biꜣt*** quarry

 ***pḥww*** marshlands, far north, distant marshlands, outer limits, ends of the earth

 ***nḥm*** rescue, take away

 ***nhmn*** surely, assuredly

 ***ḥm*** assuredly, indeed

 ***ḥm*** flee, retire, retreat

 ***ḥm*** steer

 ***ḥmy*** steersman

 ***ḥmw*** steering oar

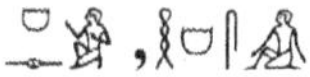 ***ḥmsi*** sit, sit down, dwell, besiege

 ***ḥmsi ḥr*** besiege

 ***ḥmsw*** sloth

 ***ḥmst*** council (of the king and courtiers)

 ***ḥmt*** woman, wife

 ***ḥmt- nṯr*** god's wife (queen's title)

 ***ẖnmt*** well

 ***sḥm*** pound, crush

 ***st ḥmt*** woman

 ***šdyt*** pool, plot of land

N - Sky, Earth, Water (cont)

42  **(5)** (as above)

O - Buildings

1 **(4)** ***pr*** *house, building, location, seat*

ꜣḫt horizon, tomb

iwyt street, house, area, sanctuary

iwnyt hall of columns

iwnn sanctuary

ibw refuge

im(ꜣ)(w) tent

imyt pr estate, property, will, testament

imnt secret place

ihw camp

iḥw stable

imḥt netherworld

itrt row of men

itḥ prison

ꜥꜥny tent, camp

ꜥfꜣy encampment

ꜥḥ, iḥ palace

ꜥt room, department

wꜣḫy palace reception hall, columned forecourt

wꜣḏyt colonnade

wmt gateway

wḫꜣ hall of columns

wsḫt hall, court

wḏꜣ magazine, storehouse

bnrw outside

bḫn tower, fortress

bḫnt pylon

O - Buildings (cont)

pr house

pri go forth

pry hero, champion

pry champion (ferocious) bull

prw excess, surplus

prw motion, procession, result

pr r ḥ3 go forth abroad

pryt house (collective)

pr ʿ energetic, activity

pr-ʿ3 Pharaoh, great house

pr ʿnkh scriptorium

pr-bity palace

pr-nbw treasury (lit - house of gold)

pr-nsw palace

pr r ḥ3 go forth abroad

pr-ẖnty harem

prt winter season

prt seed, fruit

prt procession

pr-ḏt estate

psn a loaf

mʿḥʿt, miḥʿt tomb

mnnw, mnw fortress

mht shelter

msẖn(t) resting place

mḏt stable, cattle stall

nst seat, throne

rwyt judgment hall

rwty double gate or door

O - Buildings (cont)

r-pr temple, chapel

ḥꜥ palace

ḫꜣ administrative office

ḫꜣyt portal

ḫpr become

ḫm shrine

ḫnw resting place, dwelling

ḫtm chest, storehouse

ẖnw interior

spri cause to miss, expel

sḫwy slaughter-house

st seat, place

st r occasion for speech, authority

šr stop up, close

šspt room, chamber, chapel

štyt sanctuary of god Sokar

kꜣmw vineyard, orchard

gs-pr administrative district

tp-ḥwt roof

tpḥt cavern, snake hole

ṯnnt sanctuary at Memphis

2 **(5)**

pr-ḥḏ treasury (lit - bright house)

3 **(5)**

prt-ḫrw voice (or votive) offering

4 **(2) *h***

h **room**

O - Buildings (cont)

hꜣ Ha, Ho

hꜣw environment, neighborhood, time

hꜣw neighbors, kindred

hy Hail!, shout

hp law

hmhmt roaring, war cry, squawking

hn halt

hnn deer

hrỉ be content, pleased, quiet

hrt contentment

m hꜣw in the neighborhood of, at the time of

shrỉ make content

5 **(5) *nm, mr*** *street*

mr-wr Menevis bull

mrrt street

nmỉ traverse

nmỉ lowing (of cattle)

6 **(5) *ḥt, ḥwt***

nbt-ḥt (goddess) Nephtys

ḥwt castle, mansion, temple, tomb

ḥwt nṯr temple (lit - god's house)

ḥt-ḥr (goddess) Hathor

ḥtt quarry

tp-ḥwt roof

7 **(5)** (as above)

8 **(5)**

ḥwt-ꜥꜣt temple, castle

O - Buildings (cont)

9 (5)

nbt-ḥt (goddess) Nephtys

10 (5)

ḥt-ḥr (goddess) Hathor

11 (5) *palace*

ꜥḥ, ih palace

ist palace

12 (5) (as above)

ꜥḥ palace (as above)

13 (5) *gateway, enclosure*

wsḫt hall, court

sbḫ wall in, enclose

sbḫt gateway

14 (5) (as above)

15 (5)

wsḫt hall (of palace or temple)

16 (5) ***tꜣ*** *curtain*

rmn processional shrine

tꜣ, tꜣyt curtain

tꜣyty he of the curtain

tꜣ-wr larboard, west bank

17 (5) (as above)

18 (5) *chapel, shrine*

sḳꜣ shrine base

kꜣri chapel, shrine

O - Buildings (cont)

19 (5)

itrt row of sanctuaries

itrt šmꜥ sanctuaries, or gods, of Upper Egypt

pr-wr national shrine of Upper Egypt

20 (5)

itrt row of sanctuaries

itrt mḥt sanctuaries, or gods, of Lower Egypt

ẖm shrine

21 (5)

, *sḥ-nṯr* divine booth

dmi fruit dish

22 (5) *sḥ*

, , ( ) *sḥ* booth, arbor, council chamber

sḥ counsel

23 (5)

, , , *ḥb sd* "**Sed**" festival, jubilee

sd jubilee

24 (5) *pyramid, sometimes tomb*

bnbnt pyramidion

mn nfr Memphis (LE)

, *mr* pyramid, tomb

25 (5)

, *tḫn* obelisk

26 (5) *stela, station*

, *ꜥḥꜥw* stela, station

O - Buildings (cont)

wḏ stela

27 (5) ***ḫꜣ*** *hall of columns, office*

wꜣḫy palace reception hall, columned

ḫꜣ administrative office

ḫ(ꜣ)w(y) night

ḏꜣdw hall of column, audience hall

28 (5) ***iwn***

iwn column

iwny Armant (Hermonthis) (UE)

iwnyt hall of columns

iwnyt Esna (Latopolis) (UE)

iwnw Heliopolis (ancient On) (LE)

iwnt bow

iwnt Dendera (UE)

iwntyw tribesmen

iwn(ty) sty Nubian bowman

iwn(ty)w styw Nubian bowmen

šmꜥw iwnw (Heliopolis of UE) Thebes (UE)

29 (5) ***ꜥꜣ***

iw f ꜥꜣ f one who rises in rank

iry ꜥꜣ door keeper

ꜥꜣ column

ꜥꜣ great, many

ꜥꜣ magnate, elder son

ꜥꜣ here, there, yonder

ꜥꜣ door

ꜥꜣ ass, donkey

O - Buildings (cont)

ꜥꜣ(i) be great, greatness

ꜥꜣw greatly

ꜥꜣwy r the two panels of a door

ꜥꜣb pleasant, pleasing, desirable

ꜥꜣbt self-seeking, selfishness

ꜥꜣbt food provisions

ꜥꜣbt offerings

ꜥꜣm Asiatic

ꜥꜣg flog, beat the feet of

ꜥꜣt greatness

ꜥꜣt a valuable stone, stone vessel

ynꜥm Yenoam (in Palestine)

wꜥꜣ speak abuse, curse

pr-ꜥꜣ Pharaoh, great house

ḥꜥꜣw children

ḥnyt spear

ḥꜥꜣ infant

sꜥꜣy tremble

sꜥꜣy make great, glorify

smꜣt-ꜥꜣt a fabric

29a (5) (as above)

30 (5)

sḫnt support of heaven

30a (5) ***sḏb, sdb*** *pitch fork, staff*

ꜥbt fork

mst staff

sḏb, sdb hindrance, obstacle

O - Buildings (cont)

31  (5) *ꜥꜣ door, open, instruct*

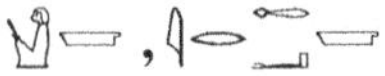 ***iry ꜥꜣ*** door keeper

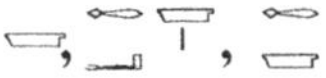 ***ꜥꜣ*** door

 ***ꜥꜣwy r*** the two panels of a door

 ***ꜥꜣmt*** Asiatic woman

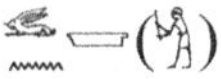 ***wn*** open

 ***wn ḥr*** instructed, expert

 ***wn ḥr n*** enlightenment is given to

 ***wḏḥ*** metal door

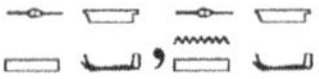 ***sn*** to open

32  (5) *door, gateway*

 ***itrt*** row of chapels

 ***bḫnt*** pylon

 ***rwt*** gate, door

 ***rwty*** double gate or door

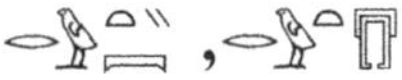 ***rwty*** outside

 ***sbꜣ*** door, entrance

 ***sbḫt*** gateway

33  (5)

 ***srḫ*** banner (for the Horus name)

 ***ispt*** throne

34 (2) ***s*** (see also **S29**)

 s she, her, it its

 ***s*** bolt

 ***s(i)*** man, someone, anyone, person

 ***sꜥb*** be equipped

 ***sꜥḥ*** mummy

O - Buildings (cont)

s nb everyone, each

sp time, occasion

sfḫw seven

sn they, them, their

sḫws make prosperous

sẖr to milk

st it, them

st, st ḥmt woman

sṯꜣw injury

sḏty child, foster child

35 (5) ***s*** (implies motion)

is go!

is ḥꜣḳ plunder

ꜥẖ brazier

ms bring, present, bring away booty, extend (aid), take aim

sy who?, what?, which?

sbi perish, be faint

sbi go, travel, conduct, spend (time), attain

sbt wrong, evil

sy who?, what?, which?

sbi go, pass, send, attain, conduct, load

sbw spoils (of war)

sb tw in search of

36 (5) *bulwark, fortification, wall*

inb wall

wmtt bulwark, fortification

mḏr shut out

O - Buildings (cont)

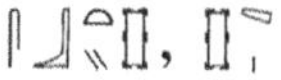 ***sbty*** surrounding wall, rampart

 ***srd*** to grow, to erect

 ***snb*** overstep, overthrow

 ***šr*** stop up, close

 ***ḳd*** builder

 ***ḏb3*** stop up, block

 ***ḏr*** wall

 ***ḏri*** wall

36a  (5) (see above)

37  **(5)** *overthrow, demolish, slanting, tilt*

 ***whn*** overthrow

 ***swhn*** tear down

 ***sẖn*** demolish (a wall)

 ***gs3*** tilt, favor

38  **(5)** *corner, angle, street, gate, magistrate*

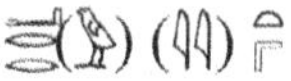 ***ʿrr(w)(y)t*** gate

 ***mrrt*** street

 ***ḥry(n)tm*** an obscure title

 ***ḳnbt*** corner, angle

 ***ḳnbt*** court of magistrates

 ***ḳnbty*** magistrate

39  **(5)** *stone, pebble, brick*

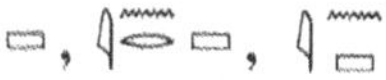 ***inr*** stone, rock, block

 ***inr ḥḏ*** limestone

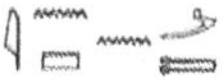 ***inr n m3ṯ*** granite

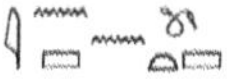 ***inr n rwḏt*** sandstone

 ***ʿ3t*** a valuable stone, stone vessel

O - Buildings (cont)

ꜥbꜣ stela, offering table

ꜥr pebble

ꜥḏ fat, grease

wꜣḏ papyrus shaped column

wdn be heavy

wdnt heavy stone

wḏ stela

biꜣ copper

biꜣ firmament, heaven

bnwt millstone

pḫꜣ pavement

mwt weight

mnw kind of stone

mḫtbt an ornament

msḳ leather

nḥp potter's wheel

rwḏt hard stone, sandstone

ḫꜣt quarry, mine

snt (statue) base block

sḫt stone patch

s(ꜣ)ṯ libation stone

sdni punish

šnsw offering stone

tit pestle

dbn deben weight

dns heaviness

ds flint

ḏbt brick

O - Buildings (cont)

40 (5) *stairway, terrace, hill*

rwdw stairway

rdw stairway

ẖtyw terrace, terraced hill, platform, dais

ṯit dais

tnṯꜣt canopy, dais

41 (5) *ascent, ascend, high place*

iʿ ascend, arise

iʿr ascend, mount, approach

ḳꜣy ascent, high place

tnṯꜣt canopy, dais

42 (5) ***šsp***

šsp receive, accept

šsp, sšp daylight

šsp palm (length), 1/7 cubit

šsp image, statue, sphinx

šspw sphinx

šspt room, chamber, chapel

šspt-dẖm chorus

43 (5) (as above)

44 (5) *office, rank*

iꜣt office, rank, function

iꜣtyw office holder

45 (5) *building*

ipt harem, private apartment

46 (5) (as above)

O - Buildings (cont)

47

(5)

nḫn Nekhen (Hieracompolis) (UE)

48

(5) (as above)

49

(5) *village, town, inhabited region, estate*

ꜣbw Elephantine (UE)

ꜣbḏw Abydos (UE)

iwny Armant (Hermonthis) (UE)

iwnyt Esna (Latopolis) (UE)

iwnw Heliopolis (ancient On) (LE)

iwnt Dendara (UE)

ipt-swt Karnak

idḥw Delta marshlands

wꜣst (nome) Hermonthis, (city) Thebes

wꜣsty the Theban forecourt

wnw Hermopolis (Ashmunen) (UE)

bꜣst Bubastis

bḥdt Behdet (LE), Edfu (UE)

p Buto (LE), belonging to Buto

pḳr precinct of Osiris at AbyDos

mniwt harbor

mn nfr Memphis (LE)

niwt village, town

n(iw)tyw those in the lower heaven

nni-nsw Heracleopolis (UL)

nbt Ombos (UE)

nḫb Nekheb (El Kab) (UE)

O - Buildings (cont)

nḫn Nekhen (Hieracompolis) (UE)

r-pr temple, chapel

rḫtt the ends of the earth

rswt south land

ḥwt-wꜥrt Avaris (LE) (Hyksos capital in the Nile Delta)

ḫm Ausim (Letopolis) (LE)

ḫmnw Hermopolis (Ashmunen) (UE)

ẖnw royal residence

ḳis city of Cusae (UE)

kmt Egypt (the Black Land)

gs-pr administrative district

ṯni Thinis

dšrt the Red Land, desert

ḏꜣtt estate

ḏdw Busiris in the delta

ḏdwt Mendes (Delta)

50 (5) ***sp*** *threshing floor, time, occasion*

ꜥšꜣ ꜥšꜣ very often

ngmgm conspire

ršršt rejoice

ḥꜣt-sp regnal year

sp time, occasion

sp-sn two times (repeat previous word)

spt threshing floor

gwꜣwꜣ fetter, bind fast, throttle, choke

51 (5)

šnwt granary

P - Boats

1 (5) *boat, ship, sail, bark, travel by water*

iw(y) one without a boat

imw boat, ship

ꜥḥꜥw ships, the fleet

wiꜣ sacred bark

wẖryt dockyard

wsẖ(t) barge

bꜣw boat

bik "Falcon" ship

mꜥnḏt bark of the dawn

mni [m] moor, land, attach, join

m-ẖdi northward

mẖnty ferry boat operator

mšꜥ expedition

nꜥi to sail, to travel by boat

nꜥt expedition

nmi traverse, travel

ns-ꜥḥꜥw overseer of ships

nšmt bark of Osiris

ḥꜥw ships, boats

ḥnw (god) Sokar's bark

ẖntit southward voyage

ẖsfi travel upstream, southward

ẖdi sailing downstream, travel north

ẖni to row, convey (by boat)

ẖnt procession (by water)

sint canoe

P - Boats (cont)

sḫnti take southward

sḳdy sail, travel by water

sḳdwt sailing

ḳ3ḳ3w boat, ship

kbnt ship

kftiw type of ship

dpt ship, boat

dpt-nṯr the divine bark

ḏ3i ferry across

1a (5) *upset, overturn*

pnʿ upset, overturn

pnʿnʿ roll over and over

2 (5) *sail upstream*

ḫnti sail (travel) southward

ḫsfi travel upstream, southward

kbnt ship

3 (5) *divine boats and actions*

wi3 sacred bark

mʿnḏt bark of the dawn

nšmt sacred boat of Abydos

sktw kind of boat

sktt bark of the evening

ḏ3i sail across the sky

4 (5) *wḥʿ* *fisherman*

wḥʿ fisherman, fowler

wḥʿ loose, stop work , return

wḥʿ unravel, explain

P - Boats (cont)

wḥꜥ distribute rations

wḥꜥ investigate

wḥꜥ ib capable, skilled

5 (5) *wind, storm, weather, sail*

iꜣb east wind

imnty west wind

ṯꜣi ṯꜣw to sail

mꜣꜥ river bank

mḥyt north wind

m mꜣꜥw nfr with a good wind, with good dispatch

nꜥw breeze

nfw skipper, captain (of boat)

nft to breathe

rsw south wind

ḥs freeze, be cold

ḥtꜣw sail

ḫt ṯꜣw mast

ṯꜣw breath, wind

ḏꜥ(w) storm

6 (5) *ꜥḥꜥ*

ꜥḥꜥ stand up, arise, erect, stand fast, attend, then, come forth, stand by, wait, at that time, in due time

ꜥḥꜥ attendant

ꜥḥꜥ quantity, wealth

ꜥḥꜥ heap, proportion, allotment

ꜥḥꜥ beer measure

ꜥḥꜥ stela, station

P - Boats (cont)

ꜥḥꜥ ib persistent

ꜥḥꜥw ships, the fleet

ꜥḥꜥw service, attendance

ꜥḥꜥw helper

ꜥḥꜥw period (of time), lifetime

ꜥḥꜥw stations, positions

ꜥḥꜥ ḥmsi pass one's life

ꜥḥꜥ ḥr indulgent

ꜥḥꜥt ships

mꜥḥꜥt, miḥꜥt tomb

nb ꜥḥꜥw wealthy man (lit - lord of heaps)

rdi ꜥḥꜥ produce

sꜥḥꜥ erect (an obelisk)

7 (5) (as above)

8 (5) ***ẖrw*** *oar*

wsr(w) oar

wsrw oars

mꜣꜥ ẖrw true of voice, justified, deceased, triumphant

ḥpt oar

ẖrw voice, cry

ẖrwy enemy

smꜣꜥ ẖrw [r] triumph [over]

smi to chastise

šd-ẖrw disturbance

8a (5) (as above)

P - Boats (cont)

9 (5) ***ḫrw-f***

ḫrw-f he says

10 (5) *steering oar, steersman*

iry ḥmw helmsman

ḥm steer

ḥmy steersman

, ***ḥmw*** steering oar

11 (5) *mooring post*

, , ***mni*** moor, land, attach, join

mniwt harbor

mnit, minit mooring post

Q - Furniture

1 (5) ***st, ws, ꜣs, ḥtm***

ꜣst (goddess) Isis

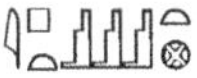

ipt-swt (the temple of) Karnak

imy st acolyte, helper

wsir (god) Osiris

bꜣst Bubastis

pḥḏw chair

mꜣst thigh, lap

nmst water jug

ḥtm perish, be destroyed

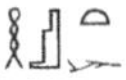

ḥtmt chair

st seat, place, throne

st-ib affection (lit - place in the heart)

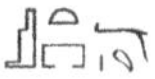

st-ns speech

st r occasion for speech, authority

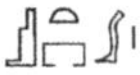

st-rd rank

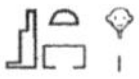

st-ḥr supervision

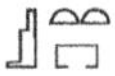

stt successor (female)

tp ḥr mꜣst in mourning (id)

2 (5) ***ws*** *chair*

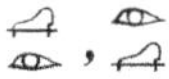

wsir Osiris

nst seat, throne

st seat

ḳꜣyt high throne

3 (2) ***p***

p mat

p base (for statue or shrine)

pis tread in (corn)

Q - Furniture (cont)

pꜥt mankind

pw that, this, whichever, who?, what?

pf, pḫy, pfꜣ that, yonder

pn this, the, he of

pꜣḳ flat cake, biscuit

pnḳ bail out

pḫꜣ split, break open, purge, clean, reveal

pẖẖ control

ptpt trample down, crush

ḥbw target

4 (5) *headrest*

wrs headrest, pillow

5 (5) *box, chest*

ꜥfdt chest

pds box

hn box

6 (5) *coffin, bury, tomb*

nb ꜥnẖ sarcophagus

ḥrt tomb

ḳrs bury

ḳrsw coffin

ḳrstt burial equipment

7 (5) *fire, hot, cook, torch*

ꜣbw to brand, scorch

ꜣm burn

ꜣẖt flame

ꜣsb fierce, glowing

Q - Furniture (cont)

ꜣšr to roast

ꜣšrt roast meat

iw-nsrsr a mythical locality

ꜥẖm quench, extinguish, destroy

wꜣi to roast

wbd(t) to burn, heat, scalded

wnmyt fire, devouring flame

wḏḥ cast (metal)

bsw flame

psi to cook

psw preparation (of food)

mꜣẖ, mꜣẖ burn, be consumed

nbi to gild, fashion

ns flame

nswt flame, fire

nsr burn, blaze

nsrt flame

rkḥ burning, heat, light

rkḥ the burning festival

rkḥ t heat

ẖt fire

sꜣm cause to burn, burn up

srf temperature

sswn destroy, destruction

sti [m] kindle, set fire [to]

sḏt flame

šsi to refine (ore)

tꜣ hot, cook

Q - Furniture (cont)

𓏏𓎡𓊮 ***tk3*** torch, candle

𓍑𓄿𓆑𓊮 ***ḏ3f*** fire, burn

R - Temple Accoutrements

1 (5) *offering table*

ḫ3t, ḫ3wt table of offerings

2 (5) *offering table*

ḫ3t, ḫ3(y)t table of offerings

3 (5) *offering table*

wḏḥw table of offerings

sš wḏḥw scribe of the offering table

4 (5) ***ḥtp*** *altar*

ḥtp altar

ḥtp rest, be pleased, satisfied

ḥtpyw non-combatants

ḥtpt bowl (for bread offerings)

ḥtpt bundle (of herbs)

ḥtpt ḏf(3) food offerings

sḥtp that pleases, that satisfies

sḥtpy censer

šnsw offering stone

dbḥt-ḥtp altar

5 (5) ***k3p, kp*** *fumigate, burn*

k3p fumigate, burn incense

k3p harim, nursery

k3p [m] cover [with]

k3p to cover, hide

k3pw roof

k3pt linen cover

kbnt ship

kpn(y) Byblus (in Phoenicia)

R - Temple Accoutrements (cont)

6 (5) (as above)

7 (5) ***bꜣ*** *incense*

bꜣ soul

bꜣ ram

nbꜣ pole

nbi to gild, fashion

sntr incense

snṯr cense, consecrate

8 (5) ***nṯr*** *god*

it nṯr god's father (priestly class)

psḏt ennead, the nine gods

nṯr god, divine

ntry, nṯr(i) be divine

nṯrt, ntrt goddess

nṯr nfr the perfect god (king's title)

ḥꜥw-nṯr the king (lit - flesh of the god)

ḥwt nṯr temple (lit - god's house)

ḥm nṯr profit, high priest

ḥm-nṯr-mꜣꜥt prophet of Maat

ḥmt- nṯr god's wife (queen's title)

sꜥḳ-nṯr god's entry

snṯr incense

snṯr cense, consecrate

šwyt god's image

gbb (god) **Geb**

9 (5)

bd natron

R - Temple Accoutrements (cont)

10 (5)

ẖr(t)-nṯr necropolis

11 (5) *ḏd*

sḏd make permanent

ḏt stability, duration

ḏd "**djed**" pillar

ḏd stable, enduring

ḏdi be stable, enduring

ḏdw Busiris in the delta

ḏdwt Mendes (Delta)

12 (5) *standard, a god*

ỉ3t standard, banner

mnw (god) Min

ḥ3 (god) Ha

13 (5) *imn* *right, west* (see also below)

imn right, right hand side

imnt west

imnti westerner (deceased)

imnty western, right hand side

imnty west wind

ḏsr-imntt Medinet Habu (lit - Western Holy Place)

14 (5) (see also above)

imnt west

wnmy right hand, right hand side

15

(5) ***iꜣb*** east, left

ꜣb n has desired

ꜣbw ivory

ꜣbḏw Abydos

iꜣb east wind

, ***iꜣby*** left hand side

, ***iꜣbt*** east, the east

, ***iꜣbty*** east, eastern

, ***iꜣbtyw*** Easterners

, ***iꜣbtyw*** the east of

iꜣbtt the East

iꜣbtt snare

16

(5)

, ***wḫ*** the nome of Cusae (UE), fetish of Cusae

17

(5)

, ***tꜣ-wr*** the nome of Abydos

18

(5) (as above)

19

(5)

iꜣtt milk

, ***wꜣst*** (nome) Hermonthis, (city) Thebes

wꜣsty the Theban

ws(r) Thebes

20

(5)

, , ***sšꜣt, sšt*** (goddess) Seshat

R - Temple Accoutrements (cont)

21 (5) (as above)

22 (5) *ḫm* (see also **O34**)

mnw (god) Min

ḫm sacred image

, , *ḫm* shrine

ḫm Letopolis (in Delta)

23 (5) *ḫm* (as above)

24 (5)

, , *nt* (goddess) **Neith**

25 (5) (as above)

80 (5)

gn (bowl) stand

ḏbꜣw altars

S - Crowns, Dress, Staves

1 (5) *crown of Upper Egypt*

- ***wrt*** great crown
- ***wrrt*** great crown
- ***nfr*** crown of Upper Egypt
- ***nfr-ḥḏt*** crown of Upper Egypt
- , ***ḥḏt*** the white crown
- ***šmꜥ-s*** the crown of Upper Egypt

2 (5)

- ***wrt*** great crown
- ***wrrt*** great crown
- , ***ḥḏt*** white crown

3 (2) ***n*** *crown of Lower Egypt*

- , ***mḥ-s*** crown of Lower Egypt
- ***n-sw-bit*** King of Upper and Lower Egypt
- ***ẖnrtt*** conspiracy
- ***sꜥḥ*** royal rank
- ***sḏꜣwty bity*** treasurer of King of Lower Egypt
- , , ***dšrt*** red crown

4 (2) (as above)

5 (5)

- ***sḫmty*** double crown

6 (5)

- ***wrt*** great crown
- ***wrrt*** great crown
- ***sḫmty*** double crown

S - Crowns, Dress, Staves (cont)

7 (5) *crown*

ḫꜥw crown

ḫprš the blue crown

8 (5) *crown*

ꜣtf **"atef"** crown

ꜣtf be crowned

ibs a king's headdress

9 (5) *double plumes*

šwty double plumes

10 (5) ***mḏḥ*** *headband, wreath*

wꜣḥw wreath

mḏḥ headband

mḏḥ hew

mḏḥw carpenter, shipwright

mḏḥt headband

11 (5) ***wsḫ*** *collar, widen*

wsḫ collar

wsḫ width

swsḫ widen, extend

12 (5) *precious metal*

nbi to swim

nbi to gild, fashion

nby gold smith

nbw gold

nbnb guard

nbt Ombos (UE)

S - Crowns, Dress, Staves (cont)

ḥḏ silver

s3wy 2/3 fine gold

ḏʿm fine gold, electrum

ddt dish

12a (5)

pr-nbw treasury (lit - house of gold)

nbw gold

ḏʿm fine gold, electrum

13 (5) *nb*

nbỉ gild, fashion

nbt Ombos (UE)

14 (5) *ḥḏ* silver

14a (5) *ḏʿm* fine gold, electrum

15 (5) *ṯḥn* , *ṯḥn*

sṯḥn make dazzling

ṯḥn gleam

ṯḥnw Libyans

ṯḥnt faience, glass

16 (5) (as above)

17 (5) (as above)

17a (5) *šsm*

šsmt malachite

šsmtt (goddess) Shesmetet

t3 šsmt a region east of Egypt

18 (5)

mnit beaded necklace (sacred to Hathor)

S - Crowns, Dress, Staves (cont)

19 (5)

- ***ns-sḏꜣwty*** chief treasurer
- ***sḏꜣw*** precious
- ***sḏꜣwty*** treasurer
- ***sḏꜣwtyw*** treasurers

20 (5) *signet ring, seal* (see also **S19** and **E31**)

- ***ns-sḏꜣwty*** chief treasurer
- ***ḫtm*** valuables
- ***ḫtm*** chest, storehouse
- ***ḫtm*** to shut, close, seal
- ***ḫtmt*** contract
- ***sꜥḥ*** be noble, rank, dignity, nobleman, worthy
- ***sḏꜣyt*** seal
- ***sḏꜣw*** rings
- ***sḏꜣwtyw*** treasurers
- ***ḏbꜥt*** signet ring

21 (5) *ring*

- ***iwꜥw, ꜥꜥw*** ring
- ***ꜥwꜥw*** ring
- ***s*** sheaf (for arrows)
- ***sšw*** metal ring or disk
- ***sdḫ*** well

22 (5) *sṯ*

- ***st(i)*** pour
- ***sttyw*** Asiatics
- ***tꜣ-wr*** larboard, west bank

S - Crowns, Dress, Staves (cont)

23 (5) *unite, proclaim, cycle*

dm pronounce, proclaim (a name), be renowned

dmḏ unite, entire, total, reassemble, bring together, accumulate

dmḏyt festival cycle

24 (5) *knot, vertebra, tie*

ṯs sandbank

ṯs saying, utterance

ṯs marshal (troops), tie, join

ṯs-pri fighting

ṯst knot, vertebra

ṯst troop, unit

ṯst ridge, range

25 (5)

ꜥw dragoman, translator

26 (5)

šndyt apron

27 (5)

mnḫt clothing, linen

ḏbꜣ (god's) garment

28 (5) *cloth, clothing, conceal, linen*

ifdy square of cloth

insy red cloth

idmi red linen

ꜥfnt (royal) head-dress

wꜣḏt green linen

wꜥbw clean clothes, sacred robe

S - Crowns, Dress, Staves (cont)

wnf be glad, happy

wt to wrap, bandage

wtꜣw wrap, bandage

pḳt. pꜣḳt fine linen

fḫ loose, release, cast off, destroy, depart

mnḫt clothing, linen

mss tunic

nms "**Nemes**" royal head-dress

nḏ thread

ḥꜣy naked

ḥꜣwy naked man

ḥꜣp conceal, hide, secret mysterious

ḥbs clothe, clothing cloth

ḥbs to bear (a ceremonial fan)

ḫn tent

smt cloth (?)

sḫrw a linen fabric

ssfw garments

kꜣpt linen cover

kf to uncover

gmḥt wick

ṯꜣwt sail

ṯnfyt sail

ḏꜣiw loin cloth

29 **(2) *s***

ꜥnḫ ḏꜣ snb life, prosperity, health (for king)

s she, her, it, its

S - Crowns, Dress, Staves (cont)

 ***s*** gold vessel

 ***s(i)*** man, someone, anyone, person

 ***s -*** prefix meaning “to cause”

 ***sy*** who?, what?, which?

 ***sip*** revise, inspect, assign, examine, destine, organize

 ***sipty*** revision, inspect, investigation

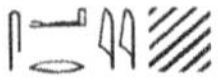 ***s‘ry*** basin on a stand

 ***sbẖt*** pylon-shaped chest

 ***sbḳ*** excellent, successful

 ***spdd*** supply

 ***spt*** ritual object

 ***sf*** mix

 ***sfw*** muddle

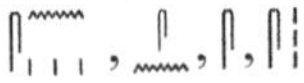 ***sn*** them, their, they

 ***sny*** those two, they two

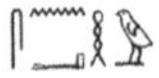 ***sn‘ḥw*** angler, fisherman

 ***snb*** health, healthy

 ***snẖn*** to control

 ***sr*** official, noble

 ***srwẖ*** tend (a patient), cherish

 ***srf*** rest, repose

 ***srẖ*** learn about

 ***shri*** make content, bring peace

 ***sḥwy*** collect, assemble

 ***sḥm*** to stop (an act)

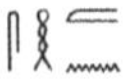 ***sḥn*** to command

 ***sẖwd*** enrich

 ***sẖmm*** make warm

S - Crowns, Dress, Staves (cont)

ssbḳ honor

ssnb preserve

sk Lo!

isṯ Lo!, behold, now

sgrḥ pacify, make peaceful

, ***st*** it, them, they

stny to crown

, ***sṯ*** scatter

sṯny distinguish, honor

sdg hidden place

sḏd relate, tell

30 (5) ***sf***

sf yesterday

31 (5) ***smꜣ***

smꜣ fighting bull

32 (5) ***siꜣ*** *piece of cloth*

() , () ***siꜣ*** recognize, perceive

, ***siꜣt*** piece of cloth

33 (5) ***ṯb, tb*** *sandal*

, ***ṯbi*** be shod

ṯbw sandal maker

, , ***ṯbwt*** sandal

, , ***ṯbwty*** pair of sandals

34 (5) ***ꜥnḫ***

ꜥnḫ sandal strap

ꜥnḫ mirror

, ***ꜥnḫ*** live, life

S - Crowns, Dress, Staves (cont)

ʿnḫ garland

ʿnḫ person, citizen

ʿnḫ captive

ʿnḫ swear, oath

ʿnḫw the living

ʿnḫw food

ʿnḫw blocks (of alabaster)

ʿnḫwy two ears

ʿnḫt corn

ʿnḫt goat

ʿnḫt (god's) eye

ʿnḫ-tȝwy Memphis

ʿnḫtt means of subsistence

ʿnḫ ḏȝ snb life, prosperity, health (for king)

wḥm ʿnḫ life (living) after death

pr ʿnkh scriptorium

nb ʿnḫ sarcophagus

sʿnḫ make to live, preserve, nourish

sʿnḫ sculptor

sḳr-ʿnḫ captive

di ʿnḫ given life

V39 (5)

tit "**tyet**" amulet

35 (5) *shade, standard*

sryt military standard

šwyt shadow, shade

šwt shade, shadow

S - Crowns, Dress, Staves (cont)

36 (5) (as above)

ḥp(wy) (divine name) Hepui

šwyt god's image

šwyt spirit, shade

37 (5)

ẖw fan

38 (5) *ḥḳꜣ* (see also below)

ꜥwt flock, herd, goats

ꜥwt "**awet**" scepter

ḥḳꜣt scepter

ḥḳꜣ rule, govern, ruler

ḥḳꜣt rulership

ḥḳꜣt "**hekat**" measure

ḥḳt (frog goddess) Heket

sḥḳꜣ cause to rule

39 (5) *ꜥwt* (also as above)

ꜥwt flock, herd (small cattle), goats

ꜥwt "**awet**" scepter

40 (5) *wꜣs, ḏꜥm, iꜣtt*

iꜣtt milk, cream

wꜣs dominion, lordship

wꜣs was scepter

wꜣsi be ruined, decay, ruin

wwꜣb(wy) the Oxyrhychite nome

ḏꜥm "**djam**" scepter

ḏꜥm fine gold, electrum

S - Crowns, Dress, Staves (cont)

41  (5) *ḏꜥm* (see also **S40**)

 ***ḏꜥm*** "**djam**" scepter

 ***ḏꜥmw*** fine gold, electrum

42  (5) *ꜥbꜣ, sḫm*

, 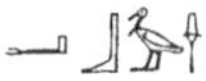 ***ꜥbꜣ*** "**aba**" scepter

,  ***ꜥbꜣ*** stela, offering table

 ***ꜥbꜣ*** offering stone

 ***ꜥbꜣ*** command

 ***ꜥbꜣ*** shine, glitter

 ***ḫrp*** baton of office

 ***ḫrp*** district, estate

, 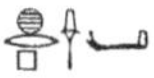 ***ḫrp*** be at the head, control

 ***ḫrp nsty*** controller of the two seats

 ***ḫrp kꜣt*** controller of works

  ***ḫrp kꜣt*** to start works or constructions

 ***sḫm*** "**sekhem**" scepter name

,  ***sḫm*** have power

 ***sḫm*** sistrum, scepter

 ***sḫmt*** power

43  (5) *md*

,  ***wḏ mdw*** to command

 ***wḏ-mdw*** to judge, litigate

,  ***mdw*** walking stick, staff, supporter

, ,  ***mdw*** speak, recite, word

 ***mdwty*** speaker

 ***mdt*** speech, words

 ***ḏd mdw in*** speech by, words spoken by

S - Crowns, Dress, Staves (cont)

 ***ḏd mdw*** speech (continued)

44  **(5)**

 ***ꜣms*** club, mace, royal scepter, staff

45  **(5)**

,  ***nḫḫw*** flail

81  **(5)** ***k*** (L)

81a  **(5)** *royal head-dress*

 ***ibs*** a king's headdress

 ***nms*** "**Nemes**" royal head-dress

82  (3) (see also **N18, X4a** and **Z8**)

 ***dꜣiw*** loin cloth

T - Weapons & Hunting

1  (5) ***mnw, mn***

 mnw mace

 ***swmnw*** Sumenu

 ***m n k*** take [to yourself] (imperative)

2  (5) ***sḳr*** *smite*

 ***sḳr*** smite

 ***sḳr-ʿnḫ*** captive incense

3  (5) ***ḥḏ***

 ***inr ḥḏ*** limestone

 ***pr ḥḏ*** treasury

 ***pḥḏw*** chair

 ***mꜣḥḏ*** oryx

 ***nfr-ḥḏt*** crown of Upper Egypt

 ***ḥḏ*** mace

 ***ḥḏ*** white, be bright

 ***ḥḏi*** to damage, injure, disobey, destroy, upset eclipse, waste

 ***ḥḏw*** onions

 ***ḥḏt*** the white crown

 ***sḥḏ*** to brighten, to light up

 ***sḥḏ*** inspector

 ***t ḥḏ*** white bread

4  (5) (as above)

5  (5) (as above)

6  (5) ***ḥḏḏ***

 ***ḥḏḏwt*** brightness

T - Weapons & Hunting (cont)

O2 (5)

pr-ḥḏ treasury

S14 (5)

ḥḏ silver

7 (5) *axe, hew*

mibt axe

mḏḥ hew

mḏḥ(w) carpenter, shipwright

7a (5)

, ***ȝkḥw*** axe

8 (5) ***tpy*** *dagger*

mtpnt dagger

tpy chief, first, first month, who or which is upon

8a (5) *dagger*

, ***b(ȝ)gsw*** dagger (see also **T8**)

9 (5) ***pḏ, pd*** *bow, stretch* (see also **T10**)

, , ***pḏ, pd*** stretch, be wide

pḏt (textile) measure

, ***pḏt, pdt*** bow, foreigners, troops

pḏt foreign bowman, foreigner

9a (5) (as above)

10 (5) ***pḏ, pd*** *bow* (see also **T9**)

iwnt bow

iwntyw styw Nubian bowmen

, ***pḏt, pdt*** bow, foreigners, troops

pḏt troop

T - Weapons & Hunting (cont)

ḥry pḏt troop commander

pḏt, psḏt The Nine Bows (a term for all of the traditional enemies of Egypt)

pḏty bowman

pḏt foreign bowman, foreigner

10a (5) *bow* (see **T10**)

Aa32 (5) *Nubia*

iwntyw styw Nubian bowmen

sty a Nubian mineral

styw Nubians

tꜣ-st(i) Nubia

11 (5) ***sẖr, swn*** *arrow*

ꜥḥꜣ, šsr arrow

sẖr overlay

swn perish

swnw physician

swnt sale

swnt price

snny chariot soldier

sswn destroy, destruction

st(i) [r] to spear, thrust [into]

šsr arrow

12 (5) ***rwḏ, rwd, ꜣr, ꜣi*** *string, bow string*

ꜣr [ḥr] restrain, hold back [from], drive away, oppress

inr n rwḏt sandstone

mꜣi(r), mꜣr wretched

mꜣi(r)w misery

T - Weapons & Hunting (cont)

 ***rwḏ*** control, administer, controller, executor

 ***rwḏ*** string, bow string

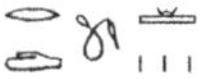 ***rwd*** strength, firmness

 ***rwḏ*** hard, firm, strong, enduring, succeed

 ***rwdw*** agent

 ***rwḏt*** hard stone, sandstone

 ***rwdt*** success

 ***rdw*** stairway

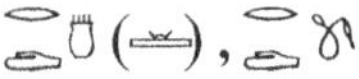 ***rd*** make to grow, flourish

 ***sm3r*** afflict, harm

 ***srd*** to grow, to erect

 ***ṯ3r*** fasten, make fast, preserve

 ***ḏ3r*** subdue, control, suppress

 ***dm3w*** groups

13  (5) *rs*

 ***rs*** be wakeful, be vigilant

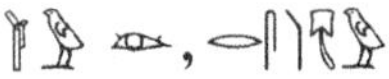 ***rsw*** sentry, vigilance

 ***rst*** foreign hoards

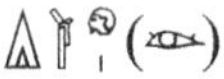 ***di-rs-tp*** foremam

14  (5) *throw stick, throw, create, form, foreign*

 ***iwntyw*** tribesmen, nomads

 ***ꜥ3m*** throw stick

 ***ꜥ3m*** Asiatic

 ***ꜥ3mw*** Asiatics

 ***ꜥmꜥ3t*** throw-stick

 ***wḥyt*** village

T - Weapons & Hunting (cont)

wḥyt tribe, tribesmen

wḏꜥ open, discern

pwntyw the people of Punt

pḏt troop

pḏt foreign bowman, foreigner

fnḫw Syrian people

mnỉ [m] moor, land, attach, join [to]

mntyw Bedouins of Asia

mryn Syrian warrior

mḥtyw northerners

mgꜣ skirmisher

mtyt rectitude

mtr fame, renown

mtr witness

mḏꜣyw Medjay from Medja

mḏꜣw Medja in Nubia

nḥsy Nubian

rs(y)w southerners

rsw sentry, vigilance

(r) pḏt foreign bowmen

rst sacrificial victims, foreign hoards

ḫꜣy plumb line

ḥbꜥ play (a game)

ḫꜣrw Khor (in Canaan)

ḫꜣst foreign land, hill country

ḫꜣstyw foreigners, desert dwellers

ḫbstyw bearded ones of Punt

T - Weapons & Hunting (cont)

ḫnwtyw skin clad people

sbi rebel

smtr bear witness to, examine, inquire

sty Nubian

styw Nubians

sttyw Asiatics

sṯny distinguish, honor

sṯs staff

ḳꜣt foes

ḳmꜣ throw

ḳmꜣ create, nature, form

ḳmḥ a loaf

kpn(y) Byblus (in Phoenicia)

tꜣ-nḥs(y) Nubia

ṯn(i) to distinguish

ṯḥnw Libya

ṯḥnt fayence, glass

ṯnw number, each, every

ṯnt difference

ḏꜣmw young men, troops

ḏʿ to spear, harpoon

ḏʿr search for, seek

15 (5) (as above)

16 (5) *scimitar, sword* (see also **T82**)

ḫpš scimitar, "**khepesh**" sword

T - Weapons & Hunting (cont)

17 (5) *chariot*

wrrt chariot

wrryt, wryt chariot

18 (5)

šms follow, accompany

šmsw follower

šmsw following, suite

šmswt following, suite

19 (5) ***ḳs, gn, twr*** *bone, harpoon, tubular*

ꜣbw ivory

wšm ear (of corn)

mꜣwt shaft

sḳsn make miserable

ḳrs bury

ḳs bone, harpoon

ḳsn be irksome

gnwt annals, records

gnwty sculptor

twr reed

twr [ḥr] show respect [for]

twri be pure

20 (5) (as above)

21 (5) ***wꜥ***

wꜥ one, unique, alone

wꜥi be alone

T - Weapons & Hunting (cont)

wˁˁw privacy, solitude

wˁˁw private apartment

, , *wˁty* sole, unique, single

wˁtt uraeus

22 (5) *sn*

sn brother

( ) , , *sn* to smell, kiss

snw pot

, *snw* two

snw companion, equal

, *snwt* flagstaffs

snsn fraternize, associate

, *snt* (statue) base block

snt sister

snṯr cense, consecrate

, , , , *snṯr* incense

, *ḳbḥ-snw-f* a son of Horus

23 (5) (as above)

24 (5) *ˁḥ, iḥ* *net, snare*

iˁḥ moon

iḥ net, snare, catch

ˁḥ wipe off, wipe away

ˁḥ net, snare, catch

ˁḥwty, iḥwty tenet farmer, field laborer (animals)

ˁḥwtyw tenet farmers, field laborers

ˁḥt field, holding, domain

T - Weapons & Hunting (cont)

25 (5) *ḏbꜣ*

- *r ḏbꜣ* instead of
- *ḏbꜣ* replace
- *ḏbꜣ* clothe, adorn, *repay, block*
- *ḏbꜣ* clothe, adorn
- *ḏbꜣ* (god's) garment
- *ḏbꜣ* stop up, block
- *ḏbꜣ* Edfu (UE)
- *ḏbꜣ-* payment, bribe, repayment, replace
- *ḏbꜣw* altars
- *ḏbꜣw* payments, rewards, bribes
- *ḏbꜣt* dressing room, sarcophagus

26 (5) *sẖt* *trap, snare*

- *sẖt* trap, snare (birds)
- *sẖt* stone patch

27 (5) (as above)

28 (5) *ẖr*

- *mẖr* storehouse
- *mẖrw* administration, governance, business
- *ẖr* under, carrying, holding, possessing
- *ẖr ꜥ* in the charge of
- *ẖry-ḥbt* lector priest
- *ẖrw* kinfolk
- *ẖrwy* testicles
- *ẖr ḥꜣt* in front of, before, formerly
- *ẖrt* portion, due

T - Weapons & Hunting (cont)

29 (5)

nmt place of slaughter

N7 (5)

ẖrt-hrw daytime

R10 (5)

ẖr(t)-nṯr necropolis

W5 (5)

ẖry-ḥbt lector priest

30 (5) *knife, sharp, cut down slaughter*

ꜣwt long knife

ꜣsẖ reap

bḥn cut off (limbs), drive off (enemy)

mds keen, alert, sharp

nkn sword

rẖs to slaughter

ḥꜣyw carrion-bird

ẖti to carve, sculpture

sꜥb to cut out, to castrate

sꜥrḳ kill

swꜣ cut off, cut down

sft sword, knife, slaughter, slaughterer

sft sacrifice

sftw butcher

smꜣ kill, destroy

smꜣ kill, destroy, smite, slay

sni cut off

T - Weapons & Hunting (cont)

šʿt slaughter, ferocity, blood lust

šʿd cut down, cut off, cut up

tp-n-sšmt specification

dm be sharp, pierce

dm sharpen

dm pronounce, proclaim (a name), be renowned

dmꜣ cut off (heads)

dmt knife

ds knife

ds flint

D57 (5) *mutilate, execute, damage*

iꜣṯ be mutilated

iꜣṯw place of execution

nkn damage, injure

siꜣty cheat

31 (5) *sšm* (See also below)

sšm guide, lead, show

32 (5) *sšm* (See above)

iry sšm functionary

sšm guide, lead, show, conduct

sšm guidance, scheme, state of affairs

sšmw divine shape, form, statue

sšmw leader, ruler

sšmt guiding serpent

33 (5)

sšm butcher

T - Weapons & Hunting (cont)

34  (5) *nm*

 *inm* skin

 *n m, in m* who, what

 *nm* knife

 *nm* go wrong, steal

,  ,  *nmi* traverse, travel

,  *nmꜥ [n]* show partiality [to], question

 *nmw* vats

 *nmḥ* be poor, deprive (of)

  *nmḥ(y)* orphan, low class person

,  *nms* "**Nemes**" royal head-dress

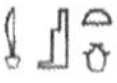, ,  *nmst* water jug

 *ẖnm* to smell , to give pleasure

,  *ẖnms* friend, associate with

 *smꜣ* kill, destroy, smite, slay

 *snm* greed

 , ,  *snm* to feed (someone), feed on, eat, supply

 *snm* to be sad

 *snm [n] [m]* to pray [to], to beg [of]

 *snmw* food supply

 ,  *tnm* go astray

 *knmtyw* those who dwell in darkness

35  (5) (as above)

81  (5) (same as **D34**,  and **D34a**, ) (O)

82  (5) *ẖpš* "**kepesh**" sword (see also **T16**)

U - Agriculture & Crafts

1 (5) ***mꜣ*** *sickle*

ꜣsḫ reap

imꜣḫ venerated state, revered, honored

imꜣḫ spinal cord

imꜣḫ venerated state

imꜣt graciousness, charm, kindliness, favor

inr n mꜣṯ granite

wr mꜣw “greatest of seers” (priestly title

mꜣ the sickle-shaped end of a boat

mꜣꜣ to see

mꜣi lion

mꜣꜥ be true, real, loyal, righteous

mꜣꜥ be offered

mꜣꜥ temple (of head)

tp mꜣꜥ accompanying, escorting

mꜣꜥ edge, brink

mꜣꜥw offering, tribute

mꜣꜣw sight

mꜣi lion

mꜣi(r), mꜣr wretched

mꜣi(r)w misery

mꜣꜥ ḫrw true of voice, justified, deceased, triumphant

mꜣꜥt truth

mꜣꜥtyw just man

mꜣw inspection

mꜣw aspect, appearance

mꜣwy, mꜣ(w) be new, fresh

U - Agriculture & Crafts (cont)

mꜣwt new thing

mꜣwt rays (of light)

mꜣwt shaft

mꜣḥ wreath

mꜣ-ḥsꜣ lion

mꜣ ḥḏ oryx

mꜣẖ, mꜣẖ burn, be consumed

mꜣ-spḥw stern

mꜣ-sḥꜣt bow

mꜣst thigh, lap

mꜣgsw dagger

mꜣṯ, mꜣt red granite

mꜣṯ, proclaim

ẖꜣbb, ẖꜣbb crookedness

simꜣ make well disposed

smꜣ scalp, locks of hair

smꜣ fighting bull

smꜣ kill, destroy, smite, slay

smꜣꜥ to offer, put in order, survey

smꜣwy renew, renovate

smꜣr afflict, harm

smꜣt union

šm(ꜣ)w wanderers, strangers, foreigners

ẖꜣb sickle

kmꜣ create, nature, form

ḳmꜣw a type of soldier

tp ḥr mꜣst in mourning (id)

U - Agriculture & Crafts (cont)

tmꜣyt mat

ṯmꜣ land survey

dmꜣ bind together

dmꜣ cut off (heads)

dmꜣw groups

dmꜣt wing

2 (5) (as above)

3 (5) (see above)

mꜣꜣ to see

4 (5) (see above)

wn-mꜣꜥ truth, reality

mꜣꜥ to offer

mꜣꜥ river bank

mꜣꜥt truth

mꜣꜥ ḫrw true of voice, justified

5 (5) (as above)

6 (5) ***mr*** *hack up, cultivate, excavate* (sometimes used as **U8** below)

ꜥd hack up

bꜣ hack up, hoe (the earth)

mr canal, channel, libation trough

mri love

mr(w) Syrian red "**meru**" wood

mrw desert

mrw harbors

mr-wr Menevis bull

mrwt will, desire

U - Agriculture & Crafts (cont)

mrrt street, avenue

mrḥ decay

mrḥt unguent, oil

mrt weavers, servants, underlings

ḥn go, depart

ḫbꜣ destroy, overwhelm

ḫbs hoe, cultivate

tꜣ-mri Egypt

7 (5) (as previous)

8 (5) ***ḥn*** *hoe* (see also **U6**)

ḥnn hoe

ḥnw "**henu**" bark

ḥnw (god) Sokar's bark

ḥnwty servant

9 (5) *measure, grain, emmer, corn*

ipt measure of 4 "**hekat**"

wꜣḥyt corn

bšꜣ malted barley

bnr date

bdt emmer

ḥḳꜣt "**hekat**" measure

ḫꜣi measure

sšr corn

šmꜥ barley from Upper Egypt

šmw harvest

šrt a grain

dḳ flour, powder

U - Agriculture & Crafts (cont)

10 (5) *grain* (see also **U9**)

ỉt barley, corn

ꜥnḫtt means of subsistence

bdt emmer

11 (5) *ḥḳꜣt* hekat measure

12 (5) (as above)

O30a (5) *sḏb, sdb* *fork*

ꜥbt pitch fork

, , *sḏb, sdb* hindrance, obstacle

13 (5) *hb, šnꜥ* *plow, seed*

, , *prt* seed, fruit

rwyt gateway, judgment hall

hꜣb penetrate

hꜣbt dance

hb plow

hbỉ tread out, travel

, (), , *hbny* ebony

hbnt “**hebnet**” (liquid) measure, a jar

, *skꜣ* to plow

, *skꜣt* cultivated land

šnꜥ repel

, *šnꜥ* magazine, storage place

šnꜥw policing

14 (5) *šnꜥ* (as above)

U - Agriculture & Crafts (cont)

15 (5) *tm*

, ***itm*** (god) Atum

, ***ḥtm*** perish, be destroyed

itmw lack of breath, suffocation

, ***rmṯ*** man, men, mankind, people

( ) , , ( ) ***ḥtm*** perish, be destroyed

, , ***tꜣ-tmw*** all men

tm complete, everything, all creation, entire, throughout

, ***tm*** not (negates verb)

tm close (mouth)

( ) , ***tmw*** everyone, all mankind

tms turn (the face)

tmt sledge

16 (5) *biꜣ* *sledge*

wns sledge

, , , ***biꜣw*** wonders, marvels

biꜣt marveling

, , , [ ][ ] ***biꜣi, by [n] [ḥr]*** to wonder [at]

biꜣty wondous person

, , , , ***biꜣyt*** wonders, marvels, miracle

biꜣi of copper

17 (5) *grg*

, , ***grg*** found, establish, snare

( ), ( )( ) , ***grg*** falsehood, lie

grgy liar

U - Agriculture & Crafts (cont)

18 (5) (as above)

19 (5) ***nw*** *adze*

msḫtyw adze

nw this, these

nw time

nw be weak, limp

nw weakness

nw see, look

nw hunter

nw care for, collect assemble

nwy return, come, bring back

, ***nwy*** water, flood

nwyt waters of a river, canal, etc.

nwḥ rope

nwḥ to bind (enemies)

nwt adze

nwd turn aside, vacillate

nwdw act improperly

nwdw unguents

nwdwt squeeze out

knʿnw Canaanites

20 (5) (as above)

21 (5) ***stp*** *cut up*

, ***stp*** choose, pick, cut up, cut off

stp dismembered, ruined

stp strip (of cloth)

, , ***stp-s3*** protect, escort

U - Agriculture & Crafts (cont)

stp -s3 palace

stpt choice

stp leap up, over leap

22 (5) ***mnḫ*** *chisel, fashion, carve*

mnḫ chisel, fashion, carve

mnḫ , be efficient, beneficent, potent, trusty, devoted, costly, excellent, splendid, thoroughly

mnḫ string (beads), fasten

mnḫw excellence, virtues

mnḫt willingness

smnḫ advance, endow, confirm, restore

23 (5) ***3b, mr***

3b stop, cease, stay, tarry, avoid

3b3b be delighted

3bi to desire

3by panther, leopard

3bw cessation

3bw elephant

3bw ivory

3bw Elephantine (UE)

3bw to brand, scorch

3bḫ [m] unite, join, mix, engage [with]

3bt family, relatives

3bḏw Abydos (UE)

mr ill, painful, sick, diseased

mr ib n be sorry for

mr ḥr ib n be displeasing to

mr a sick man

U - Agriculture & Crafts (cont)

mr pyramid, tomb

mrw painfully

mrt pains, disease

sꜣb cause to delay

sꜣb cross (water)

smr friend, courtier

smrw courtiers

Aa21 (5) *sever, judge, Seth*

wḏꜥ sever, judge

stẖ (god) Seth

Aa22 (5) (as above)

24 (5) *ḥm, ḥmw*

ḥmw be skilled, skillful

ḥmwy work

ḥmww craftsman

ḥmwwtyw craftsmen

ḥmwt craftsmen

ḥmt craft, art

25 (5) (as above)

26 (5) *wbꜣ*

wbꜣ open up

wbꜣ open courtyard

wbꜣ butler

wbꜣ (ib) (ḥr) intelligent, capable, enlightened

swbꜣ open

swbꜣ ḥr [r] initiate [into]

27 (5) (as above)

28 (5) ***ḏꜣ***

ꜥnḫ ḏꜣ snb life, prosperity, health (for king)

ꜥḏꜣ guilty man, wrongdoer

ꜥḏꜣw guilty, guilt, crime

wḏꜣ whole, sound, prosperous, uninjured

wḏꜣ be prosperous

wḏꜣ proceed, go, set out

wḏꜣ magazine, storehouse

wḏꜣ pectoral

wḏꜣ remainder

wḏꜣyt abode of Amen-Ra

wḏꜣw amulets

mḏꜣyw Medjay from Medja

mḏꜣw Medja in Nubia

wḏꜣw well-being, prosperity

mḏꜣbt one who bails out a boat

mḏꜣt papyrus scroll, book

nḏꜣ be parched, stifled

rḏꜣw fight, battle

r ḏꜣwt in return for, because of

ḥꜥḏꜣ pillage, plunder

sḏꜣ advisor

sḏꜣy ḥr divert oneself, amuse oneself

sḏꜣyt seal

sḏꜣmt pick

U - Agriculture & Crafts (cont)

ḏꜣt divert oneself, amuse oneself

ḏꜣ fire drill

ḏꜣ stretch forth, extend, reach out, take, eat, provide

ḏꜣi ferry across

ḏꜣis to contend, dispute, argue, oppose, argument

ḏꜣisw disputant

ḏꜣy ḥr divert oneself, amuse oneself

ḏꜣyt transgression, wrongdoing

ḏꜣytyw opponents

ḏꜣw night

ḏꜣf fire, burn

ḏꜣmw young men, troops

ḏꜣrw need, requirement

ḏꜣrw needs, requirements

ḏꜣhy part of Phoenicia and Canaan

ḏꜣt transgression, wrong

ḏꜣt remainder, balance, deficiency

drt, ḏꜣt hand, recite

ḏꜣdw audience hall

ḏꜣḏꜣ head

ḏꜣḏꜣ w pot

ḏꜣḏꜣt magistrates, assessors, counsel

ḏꜣḏꜣt harp

29 (5) (as above)

30 (5) ***tꜣ***

wtꜣw wrap, bandage

bt abandon, forsake, run

btꜣ run

btꜣ crime, wrong

btꜣ wrong-doer

btꜣt harm, injury

bšttyw rebels

msštꜣ frame (of chariot)

ḥnty commander

ḫt Khatti, land of the Hittites

sštꜣ mysterious, difficult, secret

sštꜣw secretly

sṯꜣ drag, draw, flow

štꜣ mysterious, difficult

sṯꜣw injury

sṯꜣw draging

, ***štꜣw*** secrets

, , ***štꜣt*** secrets

šṯyt sanctuary of god Sokar

tꜣ kiln

tꜣ be hot

, , ***tꜣš*** boundary

[ ] ***tši [r]*** be missing, stray [from]

31 (5) *baker, restrain*

itḥ prison

pr-ḫnty harem

rtḥ restrain

, ***rtḥty*** baker

, ***ḫnr*** restrain

ḫnt harem

ssnt breathe

31a (5) (as above) (O)

32 (5) ***smn*** *heavy, pound, press down, salt*

wdn be heavy

ḥmȝt salt

ḥsmn natron

ḥsmn bronze

swḏȝ make healthy, keep safe

smn press down (bread)

smn establish

smnw supports

sḥm pound, crush

dns heavy

33 (5) ***ti, t***

ipwty messenger

imsti "**Imseti**" one of the sons of Horus

ity sovereign

ityt queen regent

ʿḫnwty inner chambers, audience hall

wdnt heavy stone

mḫnty ferry boat operator

rḫt amount, number, knowledge

hr ti you are content

ḥnty horse attendant

ḥts complete, end, celebrate (a feast)

ḫnti statue

U - Agriculture & Crafts (cont)

ẖnti-ib glad of heart

ẖntit southward voyage

ẖnty-ẖty the eleventh month

ẖ3ẖti tempest

stḥn make dazzling

, ***šnty*** foe

štyt sanctuary of god Sokar

kftiw type of ship

, , ***gsty*** palette

ti "may she have"

, ***ti*** lo, behold, now

ti Ty (in Syria)

tiw Yes!

tisw stick, staff

, , , ***ti šps*** a tree, a spice

tit "**tyet**" amulet

tit pestle

[ ] ***twr [ḥr]*** show respect [for]

tnt she of

tḥnt faience

, ***ṯms*** be besmeared

ṯrt willow tree

, ***ṯḥnt*** faience, glass

34 (5) *ẖsf*

ẖsf spin

, , ***ẖsf*** repel, oppose, punish

ẖsf-ʿ oppose, opposition

U - Agriculture & Crafts (cont)

ḫsfi travel upstream, southward

35 (5) (as above)

Aa23 (5) *hit* (a mark), *follow* (path)

mḏd hit (a mark), follow (path)

Aa24 (5) (as above)

36 (5) ***ḥm***

ḥm male slave

ḥm majesty

ḥmww washerman

ḥm nṯr profit, high priest

ḥm-nṯr-mꜣꜥt prophet of Maat

ḥmt majesty (of queen or goddess)

ḥmt target stand

ḥmt female slave

D31 (5)

ḥm kꜣ "**ka**" priest

37 (5) *shave*

ḫꜥḳ shave

ḫꜥḳw barber

38 ***mḫꜣt*** balance

iwsw balance, scale

39 (5) ***ṯs*** *lift, carry, wear, balance post*

wṯst balance post

wṯs lift, carry, wear

ṯsi raise, lift up, recruit, mount, rise

U - Agriculture & Crafts (cont)

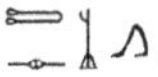, 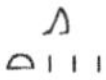 ***ṯsi*** go up

40  (5) ***rs*** *lift, carry, wear, balance post* (see also above)

 ***wṯsw*** those who have worn

 ***nhs*** to wake up

 ***rs*** be wakeful, be vigilant

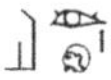 ***rs tp*** vigilant

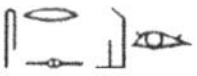 ***srs*** awaken, assume command

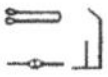 ***ṯsi*** raise, lift up, recruit, mount, rise

41  (5) *balance weight*

,  ***tḫ*** plum bob, weight

V - Rope

1 (5) **šn** *rope, drag, tie, encircle, surround*

ỉꜣdt net

ỉn (a boat's) ropes

ỉtḫ drag, draw back (a bow), remove

wꜣb cloth, swaddling clothes

wꜣt coil of rope

wꜥf bend, curb

pḥwyt stern-rope (of ship)

mnw thread

mnḫ string (beads), fasten

nwḥ rope

nwḥ to bind (enemies)

ndbw band (a door)

rwḏ string, bow string

ḥꜣtt prow rope (of boat)

ḫꜣy plumb line

ẖꜣb(t) curly appendage (on crown)

sinw ropes

swdỉ to plant

spḥw lasso

šnỉ encircle, surround, cover

šnỉ ask about, conjure

šnw network, net

šnw circuit, circumference, enclosure, cartouche

šnṯ sheriff

šnt anger, dispute

šs rope, cord

V - Rope (cont)

sšnw ropes

št 100

ḳ3bw winding (of river)

ḳ3s to bind, string

tbtb hoist

tkk attack, violate (space)

ṯs marshal (troops), tie, join

ḏdḥ imprison, shut away

2 (5) *sṯ3 hasten*

3s to hasten, to overtake, quickly, hurry, flow fast

sṯ3 drag, draw, flow

sṯ3w draging

sṯ3w injury

sṯ3t aurora (of land) (about 2/3 of an acre)

3 (5) **sṯ3w**

r-sṯ3w necropolis (of god Sokar)

4 (5) **w3**

iw3 ox

ʿw3 look after, care for

ʿw3i rob, steal, robber, one robbed

ʿw3y reap

w3i to roast

w3i [r] be far, afar, long ago, distant [from]

w3i [r] fall [into]

w3ʿw captain (of ship)

w3w lassoes

w3w wave

V - Rope (cont)

w3w3 ponder, deliberate, take council

w3w3t coil of rope, cord

w3w3t Northern Nubia, Kush

w3b cloth, swaddling clothes

w3ḥ endure, place, permit, put down, discard, overlook, ignore, set up, sit for, be patient

w3ḥ endure, place, permit, put down

w3ḥ-ib patient, well disposed

w3ḥ place, put down, permit

w3ḥ-ib patient, well disposed

w3ḥw wreath

w3ẖy palace reception hall, columned forecourt

w3s was scepter

w3sỉ be ruined, decay, ruin

w3š be exalted, be strong, be honored

w3š extol

w3g Wag festival

w3g shouting

w3t coil of rope

w3t road, way

w3ḏ papyrus

w3ḏ be green, fresh, vigorous

r w3t path, passage

bw3w magnates

w3ḏt bow (of ship)

sw3 pass by, escape, surpass, pass away, remove, transgress, occur

sw3 journey

V - Rope (cont)

swꜣ cut off, cut down

swꜣḥ cause to endure

swꜣš extol, applaud, pay honor to

šwb persea tree

šwbty a jar

šwbty ushabti figure

gwꜣ tighten, besiege, be choked

gwꜣwꜣ fetter, bind fast, throttle, choke

gwꜣt chest

twꜣ claim

twꜣ poor man, inferior

twꜣ to support, lean

dwꜣ adore, praise ~~(in the morning)~~

dwꜣt adore, praise

5 (5) **snṯ** *plan, plot out, found*

snṯ plan, plot out, found

sntt ground plan, foundation

6 (5) **šs** *clothes, tie up, pack*

isywt rags, old clothes

išst what?

ꜥrf tie up, pack, envelop, bag

mꜣḥ wreath

mss tunic

šs cord, rope

šsm leather roll

šsr arrow

sšrw linen (cloth) bag

V - Rope (cont)

sšr discuss

šst alabaster

ṯꜣm cloak, swaddling clothes

7 **(5) *šn***

šn tree

šni encircle, surround, cover

šni put down (strife)

šni suffer

šni ask about, conjure

šny hair

šnyt rain storm

šnꜥ repel, repulse, detain

šnw hair

šnw network, net

šnw circuit, circumference, enclosure, cartouche

šnw enquiry

šnw illness, disease, troubles, need

šnw encircle, enclosure, circumference

šnbt breast

šns cake, loaf

šnṯ sheriff

šnṯ revile

šnṯy foe

šnṯw fighting

8 **(5)** (as above)

V - Rope (cont)

9  (5) **šnw** *cartouche*

 ***šnw*** eternity, 10,000,000, cartouche

 ***šnw*** circuit, circumference, enclosure, cartouche

10  (5) *circuit, name*

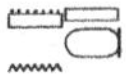 ***mnš*** cartouche

 ***rn*** name (of king)

 ***šnw*** circuit, circumference, enclosure, cartouche

11  (5) *dam, restrain, hold back*

 ***pḫ3*** split, break open, purge, clean, reveal

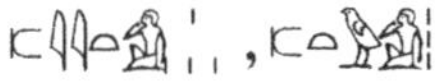 ***dyt*** shriek, bellow

 ***dni*** dam off, restrain, hold back

 ***dnit*** dam

12  (5) **ʿrḳ, fḫ** *garland, headband, loose, depart, papyrus*

 ***ʿnḫ*** garland

 ***ʿrḳ*** swear, take an oath

 ***ʿrḳ*** understand

 ***ʿrḳ*** put on (clothes), bent

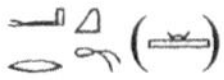 ***ʿrḳ*** know, perceive, wise, skilled, understanding

 ***ʿrḳ [n]*** bind [on]

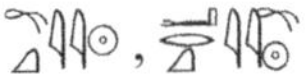 ***ʿrky*** last day (of month)

 ***wnf*** be glad, happy

 ***wnḫ*** be clad

 ***wḏ(t)*** to command, decree

 ***fnḫw*** Syrian people

 ***fḫ*** loose, release, cast off, destroy, depart

 ***mḏ3t*** papyrus scroll, book

 ***sʿrḳ*** finish, complete, put an end to

V - Rope (cont)

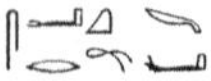

sꜥrḳ kill

sfḫ unloose, take off (clothing)

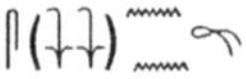

snn deed, title, copy

sḫrt papyrus roll

sš-šꜥt secretary

sšd head band, bandage

šw blank papyrus

šfdw papyrus (roll), register

ṯꜣw book

13 (2) *ṯ*

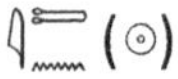

iṯn (god) Aten

ṯ you (fem)

ṯw thee, thou

ṯn you

ṯn this

ṯḥḥwt exultation

ṯswrt offering loaf

14 (2) (as above)

15 (5) (implies motion)

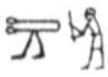

iṯi, iti carry off, seize, take possession of, remove, arrest, spend (time)

iṯi ḥpt proceed by boat

iṯw thief

bṯ, bt abandon, forsake, run

16 (5) *sꜣ*

sꜣ animal hobble, protection

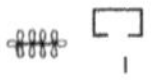

sꜣ barn

V - Rope (cont)

 ***s3*** company, regiment (of troops)

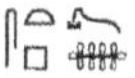, ,  ***stp-s3*** protect, escort

17  **(5) *s3***

,  ***s3*** protection

 ***imy-s3*** attendant, bodyguard

18  (5) (as above)

19  **(5) *ṯm3*** *stable, cattle stall, mat*

,  ***mḏt*** stable, cattle stall

,  ***h3r*** sack, a large measure of capacity

, ,  ***šṯyt*** sanctuary of god Sokar

 ***ḳni*** sheaf, bundle

, ,  ***ṯm3*** land survey

,  ***tm3yt*** mat

20  **(5) *mḏ***

 ***m ꜥb3*** harpoon

 ***mḏwt*** stables

 ***mḏw*** ten

 ***tp-rꜥ-mḏ*** 10 day week

21  **(5) *mḏ***

,  ***mḏ*** be deep, depth

 ***mḏt*** stable, cattle stall

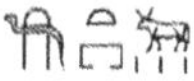 ***mḏt*** stalled cattle

M28  (5) (see **M28**)

22  **(5) *mḥ***

 ***mḥ*** fill, inlay, pay in full, make whole,complete

 ***mḥ*** sieze, hold, capture

V - Rope (cont)

 ***mḥ*** cubit (20 inches)

 ***mḥ*** be anxious

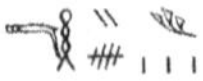 ***mḥy*** flax

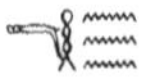 ***mḥi*** drown, launch (a boat)

 ***mḥ-ib*** be trustworthy, trusted

 ***mḥyt*** fish

 ***mḥyt*** north wind

 ***mḥw*** papyrus clump

 ***mḥt*** bowl, dish

 ***mḥt*** Delta marshes

 ***mḥt*** fan

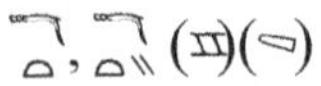 ***mḥty*** northern, northward, north

 ***mḥtyw*** northerners

 ***mḥtt*** north

23  **(5)** (as above)

24  **(5)** ***wḏ, wd*** (see also **V25**)

 ***wḏ*** stela

 ***wḏ*** jug

 ***wḏ*** inscription

 ***wḏ*** to pilot

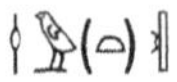 ***wḏ(t)*** command, decree

 ***wḏi*** send forth, set forth

 ***wḏyt*** (military) expedition

 ***wḏww*** wandering herds

 ***wḏb*** turn, desist

 ***wḏb*** sandbank, shore, river bank

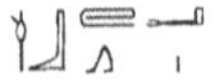 ***wḏb-ʿ*** desist, gain composure

V - Rope (cont)

 ***wḏ mdw*** to command

 ***wḏḥ*** cast (metal)

 ***wḏḥ*** pour

 ***wḏḥ*** weaned princeling

 ***wḏḥ*** wean, weaned child

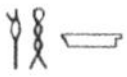 ***wḏḥ*** metal door

 ***wḏḥw*** table of offerings

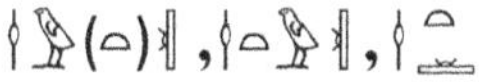 ***wḏ(t)*** to command, decree

 ***rwḏ*** hard, firm, strong, enduring, succeed

 ***rwḏ*** string, bow string

 ***swḏ* , *swd*** hand over, bequeath

25  (5) (see **V24**)

26  (5) ***ꜥḏ, ꜥd, ꜥnḏ, ꜥnd***

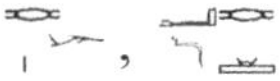 ***ꜥḏ*** spool, reel

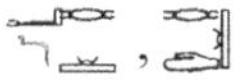 ***ꜥḏ*** be in good condition, be safe

 ***ꜥḏ, ꜥd*** perceive, recognize

 ***ꜥḏ*** hack up, excavate, cut out, destroy

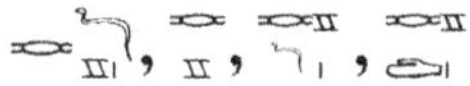 ***ꜥḏ, ꜥd*** desert edge, limit of cultivation

 ***ꜥḏ*** fat, grease

 ***ꜥḏw*** buri fish

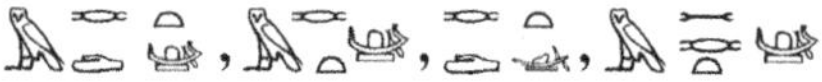 ***mꜥnḏt*** bark of the dawn

27 (5) (as above)

28  **(2) *ḥ***

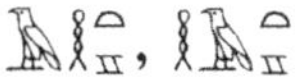 ***3ḥt*** field

 ***nḥḥ*** eternity, forever

 ***nt nḥḥ*** of (for) eternity

V - Rope (cont)

ḥꜥi rejoice, joyful

ḥw food, sustenance

ḥb feast, festival

ḥbw target

ḥbswt cloth

ḥmꜣgt carnelian

ḥsi to praise, favor, sing, honor

ḥḳr be hungry, hunger

ḥḳr hungry man

ḥkn exult, be joyful, acclaim

ḥknw exultation, praise, thanksgiving

ḥtr assess, tax, levy, provide

29 (5) ***wꜣḥ, sk*** *ward off, wipe*

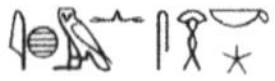

iḫm sk indestructable

wꜣḥ endure, place, permit, put down, discard, overlook, ignore, set up, sit for, be patient

wꜣḥ-ib patient, well disposed

wꜣḥyt corn

wꜣḥyt sacred space

wꜣḥw wreath, garland

wꜣḥt processional station

mꜥr be fortunate, successful

ḫsr ẖsr ward off, drive away, clear, dispel

swꜣḥ cause to endure

sk wipe, wipe out, pour out

ski perish

ski pass (time)

sky accusation

V - Rope (cont)

skw troops

skw battle, troop

sksk destroy

sktw kind of boat

sktt bark of the evening

30 (5) ***nb*** *basket*

mḏꜣbt one who bails out a boat

nb lord, master, owner (of) (used before modified word)

nb every, all (used after modified word)

nbi to swim

nb ꜥnḫ sarcophagus

nbwy the Two Lords (Seth and Horus)

nbwt Aegean islands

nbt lady

nbt basket

nbt lordship, authority

nḫbt (goddess) Nekhbet

rꜥ nb every day

ṯni basin

31 (2) ***k***

k you (masc)

kꜣ so, then

kꜣi think about, plan, so, then

kꜣt thought, plan, device, plot

ki [ḥr] cry out loud, complain [about]

kit shout of acclaim

kwi I, me, my

V - Rope (cont)

kf uncover, unclothe, strip, deprive, gather, despoil

32 (5) ***msn, gꜣw*** *harpooner*

msn Mesen (in Lower Egypt)

msnw harpooner, hippopotimus hunter

gꜣw be narrow, constricted

gꜣwt bundles, tribute, dues

33 (5) ***sšr, g*** *tie up, pack, envelop, perfume*

ꜥrf tie up, pack, envelop, bag

wgg misery, feebleness, weakness, want

sṯi, sty perfume, odor

sšr corn

sšrw things, concerns, actions

sšrw linen (cloth) bag

sšrw linen

gbtyw Coptus (in Upper Egypt)

34 (5) (as above)

35 (5) (as above)

36 (5) ***ḥn*** *receptacle*

ḥn encumber, obstruct

ḥn control, occupy, commend

ḥn receptacle

ḥnw (god) Sokar's bark

ḥnt occupation, craft

ḥnt two (both) sides (of)

37 (5) ***idr*** *bandage, bind*

idr bandage, bind, stitch, stitching

V - Rope (cont)

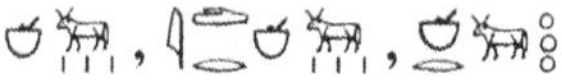 ***idr*** herd of cattle

 ***idr*** herd of elephants

 ***idr*** flock of geese

 ***idr[m]*** withhold [from]

 ***idryt*** punishment

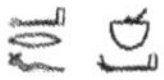 ***ꜥrf*** tie up, pack, envelop, bag

 ***ẖrpw*** mallet

 ***k3 n idr*** best bull (of the herd)

38  **(5)** *bandage, mummy cloth*

 ***wt*** bandage, mummy cloth

39  **(5)**

 ***ṯit*** "**tyet**" amulet

81  (5) ***ḳ3r*** (O)

 ***ḳ3r*** Qar (a man's name)

W - Vessels and Stoneware

1 (5) *unguent, oil*

wrḥ anoint, be anointed with

wrḥ ointment

mrḥt unguent, oil

md̠t oil, ointment

nwdw unguents

2 (5) **bꜣs** *jar*

bꜣs jar

bꜣstt (cat goddess) Bastet

3 (5) **ḥb** *feast, alabaster*

wꜣg Wag festival

psd̠ntyw, psdn, psd̠n New moon festival

msyt make a festival

hꜣkr "**Haker**" feast

ḥb celebrate a triumph

ḥb catch (of game)

ḥb feast, festival

ḥb mourn

ḥb sd "**Sed**" festival, jubilee

ḥbt ritual book

ẖry-ḥbt lector priest

sʿḳ-nṯr god's entry

snt feast of the sixth day

sḥb make festive, adorn

šs alabaster

kꜣ-ḥr-kꜣ fifth month festival

W - Vessels and Stoneware (cont)

tḫy the second month

dnỉt a festival

ḏḥwtt festival of Thoth

4 (5) ***ḥb*** *feast*

hꜣkr "**Haker**" feast

, ***ḥb*** **feast, festival**

ḥb catch (of game)

ḥby make a festival

ḥbyt festival offerings

, , ***ḥb sd*** "**Sed**" festival, jubilee

snt feast of the sixth day

sḥb make festive, adorn

sd jubilee

tp-rnpt feast of the first of the year

ḏḥwtt festival of Thoth

5 (5)

, ***ẖry-ḥbt*** lector priest

6 (5) *cauldron*

, ***wḥt*** cauldron

7 (5) ***mꜣṯ*** *red granite*

, , ***mꜣt, mꜣṯ*** red granite

mꜣṯ proclaim

, , , ***ꜣbw*** Elephantine (UE)

8 (5) (see also above)

, ***ꜣbw*** Elephantine (UE)

ꜣbt family, relatives

W - Vessels and Stoneware (cont)

9 (5) ***ḫnm*** *stone jug*

wḏ jug

nḫnm, nšnm oil vase

ḫnm join, unite

ḫnm herd

ḫnmw (god) Khnum

ḫnm(t) nurse

ḫnmt well, cistern, water source

šwbty a jar

10 (5) ***iʿb, biꜣ, wsḫ, ḥnt*** *cup*

iʿb unite, cup

(i)ʿbt ḫꜣt burial

ʿ cup

ʿʿb, iʿb cup

ʿb cup

ʿb unite

ʿbʿb to appear, to shine

wḥꜣt cauldron

wsḫ cup

wsḫ wide, broad, breadth

wsḫt broad hall, court

biꜣw rare treasures

biꜣw wonders, marvels

bit character, qualities

pgꜣ bowl

m ʿb in the company of

mḥt bowl, dish

W - Vessels and Stoneware (cont)

ḥnwt mistress

ḥnsk tie up

ḥnt cup

ḥtw bowls

ḥtpt bowl (for bread offerings)

ḫꜣw bowl

swsḫ widen, extend, enlarge

sbt laugh, laughter, mirth

sḫw width

ktwt cauldrons

10a (5) *bꜣ*

bꜣ soul

bꜣpfi (god) Bapfi

Aa4 (5) (as above)

11 (2) *g*

ipt nsw king's harim

ꜥgn pedestal

b(ꜣ)g(i) be remiss, slack

nst seat, throne

snw pot

sgnn soften, weaken

sgrḥ pacify, make peaceful

sdgꜣ r hide from, conceal from

sdgi hide

sdgw hidden things

gy an offering loaf

gwg shout

W - Vessels and Stoneware (cont)

gn (bowl) stand

gnn soft, weak

, ***grg*** found, establish, snare

, ***grt, gr*** older, moreover, now, further, either

, ***dšrt*** red pot

) ***dgi*** hide

12 (5) (as above for seat)

13 (5) (as above for red pot, see also **N34**)

14 (5) ***ḥs*** *jar*

ḥs freeze, be cold

ḥs turn back

(), , , ***ḥsi*** to praise, favor, sing, honor

, ***ḥsy*** favored one, honored one

ḥsyt concubine

() ***ḥsw*** singer

ḥswt praises, favors, honors

ḥswti favorite

ḥs ḥr.f courageous

, ***ḥst*** water pot

ḥsty praise

m-ḥis to face someone (aggressively)

sbt libation jar

, () ***snbt*** jar

15 (5) ***ḳb, ḳbḥ*** *cool, libation*

wdḥ pour out, pour off

ḳb scatter

ḳbb be cool

ḳbḥ fountain

ḳbḥ libate, libation

ḳbḥw sky

ḳbḥ-snw-f a son of Horus

ḳbḥt libation vase

16 (5) ***ḳb, ḳbḥ*** (also as above)

ḳbḥ death

ḳbḥw libation, cool water

ḳbḥw libation vase

17 (5) ***ẖnt***

imy ẖnt priestly title

m ẖnt within, out of

ẖnt first, foremost, in front of, (go) forth, among, from

ẖnt face

ẖnti sail (travel) southward

ẖnti-ib glad of heart

ẖntit southward voyage

ẖnty crocodile

ẖnty in front of

ẖntyw tenants

ẖntyw-tȝ Southerners

ẖnty-ẖty the eleventh month

ẖntyt sail (travel) southward

ẖntw racks for water pots

sẖnti advance, promote

sẖnti take southward

ẖnt š wooded country, garden

W - Vessels and Stoneware (cont)

18  (5) (as above)

19  (5) *mi* *milk jug*

 ***3mi [ḥr]*** mix, compound [with]

 ***idmi*** red linen

, ,  ***mi, mr*** like, as well as, according to, as when, according as

 ***mi*** (someone's) equal

 ***miw, mit*** cat

 ***mi m*** how?

,  ***min*** today

,  ***my, mi*** likewise, accordingly

 ***miḫt*** the like

 ***mit(y)*** copy

 ***mity*** likeness

 ***mitt*** likeness, the like

 ,  ***mity, mitw*** like, equal

 ***m-mitt*** likewise

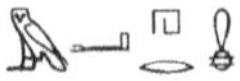 ***mhr*** milk jug

 ***r-mitt-irw*** as well as

 ***smi*** to chastise

 , ***smi*** to report, announce, proclaim, acknowledgement

 ***ḳmi*** apply resin or gum to

 ***ḳmi spt*** reluctant

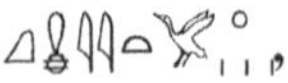, ,  ***ḳmyt*** gum, resin

,  ***dmi*** town

20  (5) *milk*

, ,  ***irtt, irṯt*** milk

21  (5)  ***irp*** wine

W - Vessels and Stoneware (cont)

22 (5) *beer, pot, measure, vessel, drunken*

iꜣtt milk, cream

inw tribute

ꜥḏ fat

wšmw beer jar

wdpw butler

bit honey

mrḥt unguent, oil

mni measure of capacity

mḥt bowl, dish

rhdt jar, vat, cauldron

ḥnw vessel

ḥnḳt beer

sṯt beer jar

šꜣbw food, meals

ḳrḥt vessel

tḫ(i) be drunken

tḫt drunkenness

ds beer jug, "**des**" (measure)

23 (5) (as above but not just **beer**)

inw produce, quarry, gifts, tribute

ꜥntyw myrrh

wrḥ anoint, be anointed with

bꜣḳ moringa oil

wdpw butler

mni pot

mnḳt jar

W - Vessels and Stoneware (cont)

nw produce, quarry, gifts, tribute

nmst water jug

(…) ***hbnt*** "**hebnet**" (liquid) measure, a jar

ḳrḥt vessel

ḳḥ jar

24 (3) *nw, in* *pot*

iꜣꜥnw lamentation, sorrow, woe

iꜥn baboon, sacred baboon

inw produce, quarry, gifts, tribute

inn we

ink I, me, my

ꜥnw averted

ꜥẖnwty inner chambers, audience hall

ꜥš cedar, pine, fir

wnw Hermopolis (Ashmunen) (Upper Egypt)

wnwt hour, priestly duties

wnwt priesthood

wnwt(y) hour watcher, astrologer

wdnw offerings

wḏḥ pour

bṯnw, btnw defiant man, rebel

fnfnw award compensation

mnw monument

mnw trees, forest

mnnw, mnw fortress

mhr milk jug

msnw harpooner, hippopotimus hunter

W - Vessels and Stoneware (cont)

mtnwt reward

nìw, nww, nw, nnw, nwnw primeval waters

nw, nyw of

nwk I, me, my

nwt (goddess) Nut

nḫbt (goddess Nekhbet)

nḏ protect

nḏ ask

rnnwtt harvest goddess, name of ninth month

hy hnw jubilate

hnw jubilation, praise

hnw neighbors, associates, family

ḥnw vessel

ḥnwt mistress

ḥnḳt beer

[ḥr] snw [sy] [for] another [time]

ḥknw exultation, praise, thanksgiving

ẖnw resting place, dwelling

snw companion, equal

sḳdi sail, travel by water

sḳdw saior, traveller

šbnw various

špnt beer measure

šnw net

ṯnwt number, quantity

ṯnw number, each, every

ḳd build, fashion (pots)

W - Vessels and Stoneware (cont)

ḳd form

tpt fine oil

tfnt (goddess) Tefenet

ṯbt vase

ṯpḥt cavern, snake hole

ṯnwt, ṯnwt quantity, number

ṯnwt number of cattle

ṯnwt number of prisoners

ṯnwt r greater amount than

ṯḥnw Libya

ṯḥnt faience, glass

ḏnwt families

ḏꜣḏꜣ w pot

ḏꜣḏꜣt magistrates, assessors, counsel

ḏnw flaw

25 (5) *in*

in(i) bring, fetch, remove, carry off, bring about, overcome, reach, attain

inyt refrain (of song)

inw produce, quarry, gifts, tribute

inw matting

inw pattern, model

80 (5) *jar*

ḳby beer jar

ṯꜣb a jar

81 (5) *dish*

ddt dish

X - Loaves and Cakes

1 (2) *t*

t bread

-t (infinitive - suffix)

-t you (fem), feminine (suffix)

it father

it.f his father

t3 this, the, she of

t3y i my

ty forsooth, pray

-ty (fem. dual suffix) very, two, pair of

tw one, someone, this, that, these, those

twt statue, image, figure

twt pleasing, fair, fitting, like

tf that, yonder

tfy upon, when

tn you

tn this

M5 (5) time, season

ti, tr time, season

2 (5) *food, bread*

inpw (god) Anubis

wnmw food, sustenance

prt-ḫrw invocation offerings

ḥ3w-ḫt special offering

ḥtp(w)-nṯr divine offerings

ss3w provisions, sustenance

š3bw meals, food

X - Loaves and Cakes (cont)

šns cake, loaf

ḳw loaf, cake

ḳmḥ a loaf

gb (god) **Geb**

t bread

t ḥḏ white bread

ḏḥwty (god) Thoth

3 (5) (as above)

4 (5) ***sn*** *food , rites, invocation, reward* (see also **X5**)

isnii are opened

pꜣḏ a loaf

prt procession

prt-ḫrw invocation offering offerings

fḳꜣ cake

fḳꜣ reward

rkḥ the burning festival

ḥbw festivals

ḫfꜥt food

snw food

t bread

ḏnb a offering loaf

4a (5) *cake, food, provisions* (See also above and **N18, S82** and **Z8**)

ꜣwt , ꜣwt ꜥ gifts, offerings

ꜥꜣbt food provisions

ꜥnḫw food

ꜥḳw provisions, revenue (in food), loaves

wnmw food, sustenance

X - Loaves and Cakes (cont)

wnmt food

ßw food supplies

msyt supper, evening meal

nsty a type of bread

rdniw share, portion

ḥw food, sustenance

ḥry-ẖt-f offering loaf

ḥrf kind of bread

ḥtpt ḏf(ꜣ) food offerings

snmw food supply

šꜣbw food, meals

šbw food, meals

šns cake, loaf

ḏf(ꜣ) provisions

dniw share, portion

drpw offerings

5 (5) ***sn*** *provisions, food, bread*

ꜥḳw provisions, food

m snt r in the likeness of, in accordance with

snỉ to surpass, pass by

snny chariot soldier

t bread

6 (5) ***pꜣt*** *loaf*

pꜣt bread offering, loaf

pꜣt primeval times, antiquity

pꜣwty primeval god

X - Loaves and Cakes (cont)

psḏntyw, psdn, psḏn New moon festival

7 (5) *food* (see also **N29**)

wnm eat

wšb eat

pḏw spread out

snw food offering

gsw half-loaves

8 (5)

imi to give

rḏw efflux

di(w) provisions

di, rdi to give

di(w) gift, gratuity

di ꜥnḫ given life

di-rs-tp foreman

dḳ(r) fruit

ḏdw Busiris in the delta

80 (5) *bread*

ḏꜥ type of bread

Y - Writing and Games

1

(1) **mḏ3t** *writing, abstract notions*

ip to count, calculate, reckon, access, pay, examine, heed, assemble

ipt reckoning, census

ip ḏt. f grow up (id) (lit - count his self)

iẖ then, therefore

išt property, belongings

iḳr excellent, precious, virtue

ʿ3 great

m3ʿt truth

m3w(y) be new

m(w)dt word

mḏ3t papyrus roll, book

( ) **mḏ3t** sculptor's chisel

n iḳr by virtue of

r iḳr exceedingly

rẖ know, learn

ḥk3 magic

siḳr advance, promote (a person), adorn (a place)

sš write

dmd total

1a

(1) (as above)

2

(1) (as above)

2a

(1) (as above)

3

(5) **sš** *scribe's outfit, smooth, ground fine, red, injury*

mnhd scribe's outfit

( ) **nʿʿ** smooth

snʿʿ made smooth, ground fine

Y - Writing and Games (cont)

sš scribe

, ***sš*** to write

sšw writings

sš-šꜥt secretary

ṯms red

, ***ṯms*** be besmeared

ṯmsw injury, harm

4 **(5)** (as above)

5 **(4)** ***mn***

imn (god) Amun

, ***imn, imnt*** hide, secret, conceal

imnyt daily offerings

imnt secret place

inhmn pomegranate

, ***mn*** remain, be firm, be established, enduring, be fixed, stick fast, be attached, be vested

m mn at the rate of

mn be ill (of), suffer (from), miserable (about), troubled (about)

mn sick man

, ***mn, mnt*** so and so, someone, such a one

mnt such an amount, the like

, ***mnꜥ*** to nurse, suckle

mnꜥy male nurse, tutor

mnꜥt nurse

mnꜥt nurse, foster mother

mni pot

, ***mni*** measure of capacity

, ***mni*** death, die

Y - Writing and Games (cont)

mniwt harbor

mniw herdsman, assault troops

mni [m] moor, land, attach, join [to]

mnit mooring post

mnit necklace (sacred to Hathor)

mnꜥt milk cow

mnw monument, memorial

mnw trees, forest, plantation

mnw kind of stone

mnwy abundant of monuments

mnwt pigeon

mnfyt, mnfꜣt soldiers, assault troops

mnfrt (arm) band

mnmn move about, be disturbed

mnnw, mnw fortress

mn nfr Memphis

mnḥ wax

mnḥ papyrus plant

mnḥw froth

mnḫ be joyful

mnḫ , be efficient, beneficent, potent, trusty, devoted, costly, excellent, splendid, thoroughly

mnḫ chisel, fashion, carve

mnḫ , be efficient, beneficent, potent, trusty, devoted, costly, excellent, splendid, thoroughly

mnḫ string (beads), fasten

mnḫt the third month

mnḫt clothing, linen

mnš cartouche

Y - Writing and Games (cont)

mnḳt jar

(m) mnt daily

mnt swallow (bird)

mnt thigh, haunch

mnṯyw Bedouins of Asia

mnḏ, mnd breast

rmn total

r mn together with, as well as

r mn m as far as

rmn arm, shoulder, side, to carry

ḥsmn bronze

smn preserve, record, make firm, fortify

smnw supports

smnḫ advance, endow, confirm, restore

smnmn shift

smntyw emissaries

6 (5) *ibꜣ*

ib(ꜣ) to dance

ibꜣ senet game piece

ibꜣ(w) dances

7 (5) *harp*

bnt harp

8 (5) *sḫm* *sistrum*

sḫm ir(y) f potentate

sššt sistrum

Z - Strokes, Signs, Figures

1 (1)

wꜥ one, unity , (actual thing depicted)

2 (1) ***w***

w (plural indicator)

3 (1) (as above)

N33 (3) (as above)

4 (2) ***wy***

wy two, duality, (sometimes used for)

sny those two, they two

5 (5) (replacement for dangerous or complex signs)

ꜣt attack, moment, striking power

iꜣdt, idt dew, pouring rain

iꜣdt net

biꜣyt wonder, marvel

mt strip (of cloth)

smdt subjects, subordinates, staff

6 (5) *die, enemy*

ꜣw death

ꜥꜣm throw stick

mt die, death

ẖpt decease

ẖft(y) enemy

7 (2) ***w*** (abbreviation of **G43**, see also **V1**)

w they, them, their

Z - Strokes, Signs, Figures (cont)

8 (3) *round, circuit* (see also **N18,S82** and **X4a**)

sn reveal

sni to pass by

šnw round, circuit

šnw network, net

šnw circuit, circumference, enclosure, cartouche

N33 (3) *builders, round, character* (see also **W24, N33,** and **D12**)

iḳdw builders

mt die, death

ḳd character

M44 (5) *thorn, sharp, bread*

spd sharp

srt thorn

t-ḥḏ white bread loaf

9 × (4) *damage, divide, lessen, cross, answer, et al*

ꜣbẖ [m] unite, join, mix, engage [with]

ipt mission, message, occupation

ipwty messenger

wbẖ be bright

wpi divide, part, open, judge, discern, distinguish

wpy decision

wp st specifically

wpš strew, scatter

wpt specification

wpt st specifically

whn overthrow

wšb answer

Z - Strokes, Signs, Figures (cont)

wšbw comforter

wdỉ throw, shoot (an arrow), extend

wdỉ to make (sound)

btꜣ wrong-doer

btꜣt harm, injury

pss results of labor

psš divide

psš division

psšt sharing out, share, portion, apportioning

ptpt trample down, crush

fdỉ to pluck

fdḳ tear asunder, piece, fraction

mnỉ measure of capacity

nft loose, slacken

nḥb yoke together, unite

nẖb open (for use)

nẖb stipulation

nẖb fresh land

nẖbt titulary, protocol

nkt matter, trifle, little

ngỉ break open

ngt breach

rmrm chastise

r ḏꜣwt in return for, because of

ḥsb reckon

ḥsb 1/4

ḥḏỉ to damage

ẖbꜣ destroy, overwhelm

Z - Strokes, Signs, Figures (cont)

ẖbi to lessen, subtract

ẖbn be guilty, distorted

ẖbsw cultivated lands, plowlands

sw3(i) to pass by, escape

sw3 cut off

sw3i pass by, escape, surpass, pass away, remove, transgress, occur

sw(r)i drink

sn to open

sš spread out, pass

sḏt flame

sḏ(i) to break

šbi to change, alter, mix, mingle, confuse

šbn [ḥr] mixed [with]

šbnw various

šbsb regulate, transform, adjust, divide

šnš tear up

št (tax) assessment

ktkt quiver

ḏ3t divert oneself, amuse oneself

gmgm break

t3š boundary

tš smash, grind, split

tši [r] be missing, stray [from]

ḏ3 fire drill

ḏ3 stretch forth

ḏ3i to cross, ferry across

ḏ3y ḥr divert oneself, amuse oneself

, ***ḏ3yt*** transgression, wrongdoing

, ***ḏ3ytyw*** opponents

ḏ3t transgression, wrong

10 (5) (as above)

11 (5) ***imi, wn*** (see also **E34** and **M42**)

imi not be (negation)

, , ***imy*** who (which) is in, being in

, ***imy is*** councilor

, ***imy wrt*** west side, starboard

imy b3ḥ who is in the presence, who existed before time, ancestor

imy rn f list of names

imy ḥ3t who (which) is in front, prototype, pattern, mold, example

imy ẖnt priestly title

(), , ***imy ẖt*** who follows, accompanies, bodyguard, attendant, posterity

imy s3 attendant, bodyguard

, , ***imytw*** between, among

imyt pr estate, property, will, testament

, ***imy-ib*** favorite

imyw-ḥ3t ancestors flame

, ***imt pr*** estate, property, will, testament

imt nḏst (boat's) stern

imt ḥ3t f uraeus

, ***wnm*** eat

wnmyt fire, devouring flame

() () ***(m) (r) imytw*** between, among

Aa - Unclassified

1 (2) *ḫ*

ḫ placenta

ḫbd to blame, disapprove of, be hateful

ḫfʿ a cake

ḫfʿ seize, grip, grasp

ḫft in front of, as well as, corresponding to

ḫnp rob, despoil, offer

ḫnmt red jasper, carnelian

ḫnrwt women of the harem

ḫns traverse

ḫr under (king), with, near, to, by, and, further

ḫrp at the head, in front, control, administer

ḫrpw mallet

ḫt thing(s), anything, matter, affair

ḫft in front of, as well as, corresponding to

ḫdt land register

2 (5) *wt, ḫp, wḥ3, g3* *bodily growths or condition, suffer, would, disease, fat, excrement, odor, clay, granite, cedar*

3bw Elephantine (UE)

(i)ʿbt ḫ3t burial

iwtyw corruption

ʿš cedar, pine, fir

wbnw wound

wh3t , wḥt cauldron

wḥ3t , wḥt oasis

wḫd suffer, bear patiently, pain

wt to wrap, bandage

wt embalmer

Aa - Unclassified (cont)

mꜣṯ, mꜣt red granite

nḥꜣ be hard, rough, dangerous, contrary, perverse

rḏw efflux

ḥs excrement

ḥsb reckon

ḥsb workman

ḥsbw doom

ḫꜣyt disease, illness

ẖpn fat

ẖrt state, condition, requirements, products

ẖꜣt corpse

ẖpꜣ navel, umbilical

ẖpw sculptured reliefs

sꜣ weak

sin clay

srwḫ tend (a patient), cherish

sṯi, sty perfume, odor

sṯꜣw injury

šfw swell

sdwḫ treat, embalm

gꜣw be narrow, lack, deprive

gꜣwt bundles

tp-ḥsb reckoning, norm, standard, rectitude

ḏꜣrw needs, requirements

ḏdꜣ fat

3 **(5)** *soft or liquid anatomical matter* (see also **Aa2**)

ꜣs soft inner body parts

wsšt urine

Aa - Unclassified (cont)

sṯ odor

4 (5) ***bꜣ***

bꜣ soul (see **W10**)

5 (5) ***ḥp***

iṯi ḥpt proceed by boat

ḥip hasten

ḥp Apis bull

ḥpy (god) Hepy (son of Horis)

ḥpw Apis bull

ḥpwty runner

ḥpt oar

ḥpt boat

dsr ḥpwt direct the boat, sail

6 (5) ***ṯmꜣ***

ṯmꜣ land survey

ṯmꜣyt mat

7 (5) ***sḳr*** *smite*

sḳr smite

sḳr captive

sḳr-ꜥnḫ captive

7a (5) (as above)

8 (5) ***ḏꜣ, ḳn*** *district, estate*

ꜥḏ desert edge

ns pr n ḏꜣtt steward of the estate

spꜣt district

smt desert, necropolis

ḳn complete, be completed

Aa - Unclassified (cont)

ḳn mat

ḏꜣtt estate

ḏꜣḏꜣt magistrates, assessors, counsel

9 (5) *rich*

ḫwd rich

10 (5)

drf writing

11 (5) *mꜣꜥ*

wn-mꜣꜥ truth, reality

mꜣꜥ send dispatch

mꜣꜥ ḫrw true of voice, justified, deceased, triumphant

mꜣꜥt truth

mꜣꜥtyw just man

m mꜣꜥw nfr with a good wind, with good dispatch

smꜣꜥ ḫrw [r] triumph [over]

ṯntt raised platform

11a (5) (as above)

12 (5) (as above)

12a (5) (as above)

13 (2) *m, ỉm, gs* (See also G17)

ỉm a body part

ỉmỉ to give

ỉmw certain body parts

ỉmw boat

m in, as, by, with, from, when, through (etc.)

Aa - Unclassified (cont)

mki guard, protect, look after

rdi ḥr gs partial, bias, dispose of, kill

gs side, half, border, lay low (an enemy)

gs anoint

gs-pr administrative district

gs-ḥry top, uppermost

gst speed

gsty palette

14 **(2)** (as above)

15 **(2)** (as above)

16 **(5)** ***gs***

ḫm shrine

gs side, half, border, lay low (an enemy)

17 **(5)** ***sꜣ*** (see also Aa18)

mꜣ-ḥsꜣ lion

rdi ib m-sꜣ be anxious about

ḥry-sꜣ a breed of cattle

sꜣ back

sꜣ weak

sꜣ barn

sꜣi be satiated

sꜣwt walls

sꜣmt mourning

sꜣr be wise

sꜣḥ grant, endowment

sꜣḥ land grant

sꜣḥ toe

Aa - Unclassified (cont)

sꜣḥ approach, reach, arrive at, kick

sꜣḥ (constellation) Orion

sꜣḥw neighbors, dependents

sꜣḥt neighborhood

sꜣsꜣ to force, repel

, **sꜣsꜣ** repel, force (boat), overthrow

ssꜣi satisfy, make wise

ssꜣw provisions, sustenance

sṯꜣ drag, draw, flow

šsꜣ be skilled

gsꜣ tilt, favor

gsꜣ favorite

18 (5) (as above)

19 (5) **ḥr** *prepare, preserve*

ḥr prepare

() [] **ḥr [r]** be far, distant [from]

ḥryt dread

ṯꜣr preserve

20 (5) **ꜥpr**

, **ꜥpr** equip, provide, acquire, incur, man

ꜥprw equipment

ꜥprw sailors

ꜥprw workmen

ꜥprw jewelry

21 (5) *sever, judge*

, , , **wḏꜥ** divide, sever, judge between

Aa - Unclassified (cont)

wḏꜥ-rwt judge

wḏꜥt judgment

wḏ-mdw to judge, litigate

stẖ (god) Seth

ḏꜥr, ḏꜥ search out, seek

22 (5) (as above)

23 (5) *hit, adhere*

mḏd hit (a mark), stay on (a path)

24 (5) (as above)

25 (5)

smꜣ priest who clothes the god

26 (5) *rebel*

sbi rebel

27 (5) ***nḏ***

inḏ ḥr hail to

nḏ ask, inquire

nḏ protect

nḏ thread

nḏ grind

nḏ ḥr confer [on], greet

nḏ [m ꜥ] save [from]

nḏw miller

nḏwt r counsel, consultation

nḏnḏ take counsel

nḏ r take counsel, consult, question

nḏ ḥr greet

nḏ ḥr gifts, homage

nḏ ẖrt greet, pay one's respects,

nḏty protector

nḏtyw maid-servants

snḏ fear

28 (5) ***ḳd***

mw-pf-ḳdw the Euphrates River

sḳd cause to build

sḳdy sail, travel by water

sḳdw sailor, traveller

sḳdwt sailing

sḳdwt company of troops

ḳd build, fashion (pots), form

ḳd builder

ḳd go round

ḳdw enemies from Kode

ḳdtt a Syrian tree

ḳdwt drawings

29 (5) (as above)

30 (5) *adorn, decorate, ornament*

ḥts complete, end, celebrate (a feast)

ẖkr be adorned

ẖkryt nsw king's ornament (concubine title)

ẖkrw ornament, insignia

ẖkrt concubine, hairdresser

31 (5) (as above)

Aa - Unclassified (cont)

32  (5) *Nubia*

 ***iwn(ty) sty*** Nubian bowman

 ***iwntyw styw*** Nubian bowmen

,  ***sty*** a Nubian mineral

 ***sty*** Nubian

, 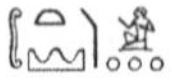 ***styw*** Nubians

, 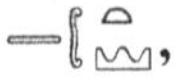, 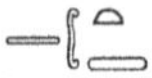, 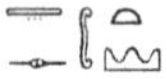 ***tꜣ-st(i)*** Nubia

80  (5)

 ***sdni*** punish

 ***kbnt*** ship

 ***dni*** dam off, restrain, hold back

Index to Sign List

A - Man and Occupations

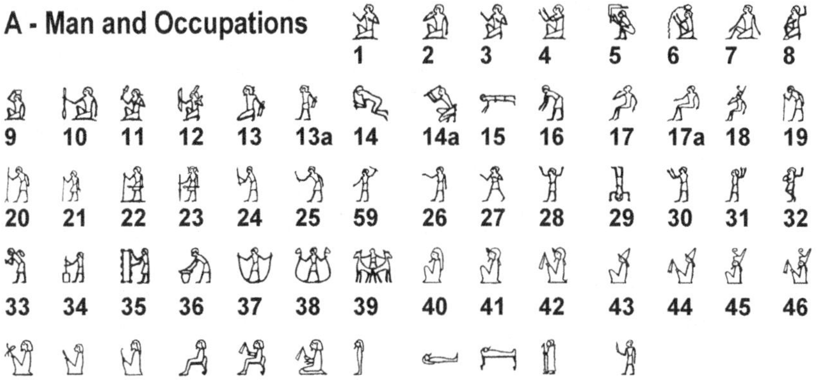

1 2 3 4 5 6 7 8
9 10 11 12 13 13a 14 14a 15 16 17 17a 18 19
20 21 22 23 24 25 59 26 27 28 29 30 31 32
33 34 35 36 37 38 39 40 41 42 43 44 45 46
47 48 49 50 51 52 53 54 55 81 82

B - Woman and Occupations

1 2 3 4 5 6 7

C -Deities

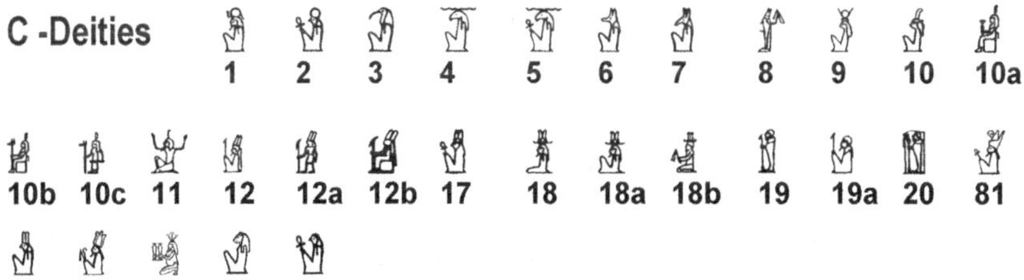

1 2 3 4 5 6 7 8 9 10 10a
10b 10c 11 12 12a 12b 17 18 18a 18b 19 19a 20 81
82 83 85 86 87

D - Human Body Parts

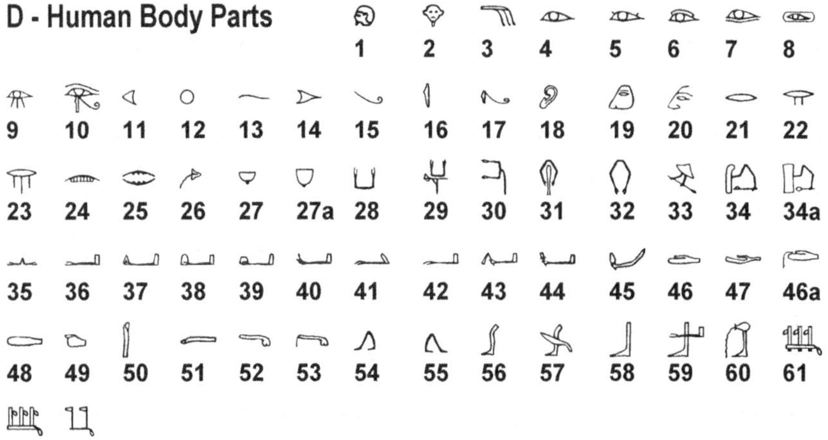

1 2 3 4 5 6 7 8
9 10 11 12 13 14 15 16 17 18 19 20 21 22
23 24 25 26 27 27a 28 29 30 31 32 33 34 34a
35 36 37 38 39 40 41 42 43 44 45 46 47 46a
48 49 50 51 52 53 54 55 56 57 58 59 60 61
62 63

E - Mammals

F - Mammal Parts

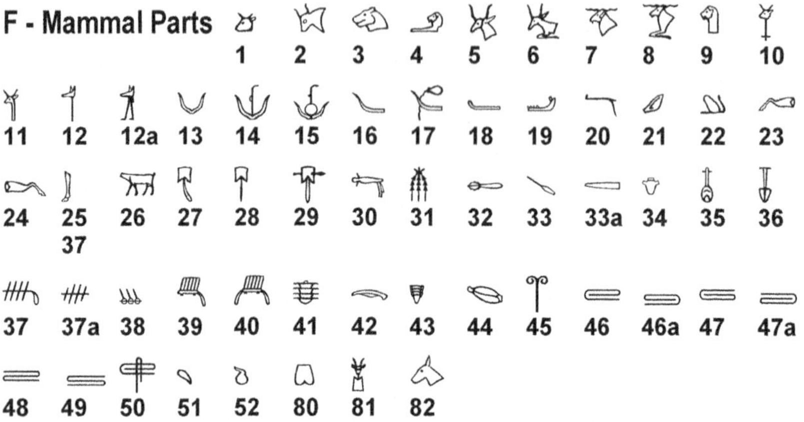

G - Birds

H - Bird Parts

I - Reptiles, etc

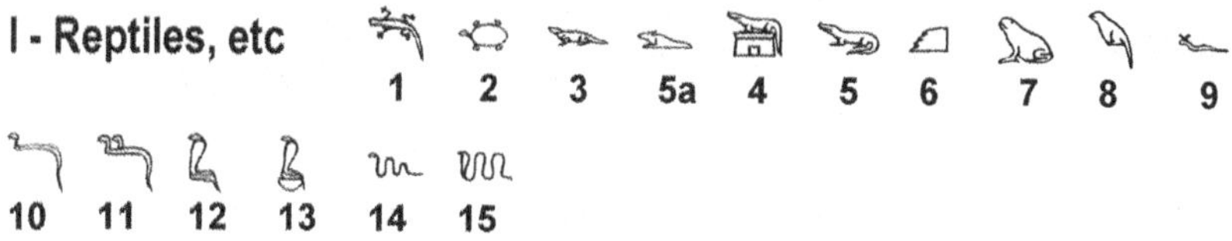

1 2 3 5a 4 5 6 7 8 9
10 11 12 13 14 15

K - Fish and Parts

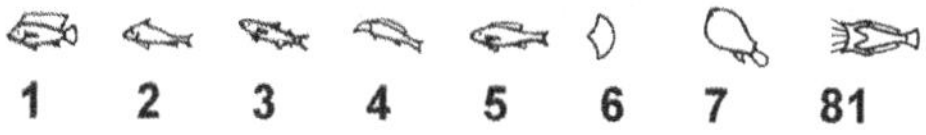

1 2 3 4 5 6 7 81

L - Misc Annimals

1 2 3 3a 4 5 6 7 81

M - Plants

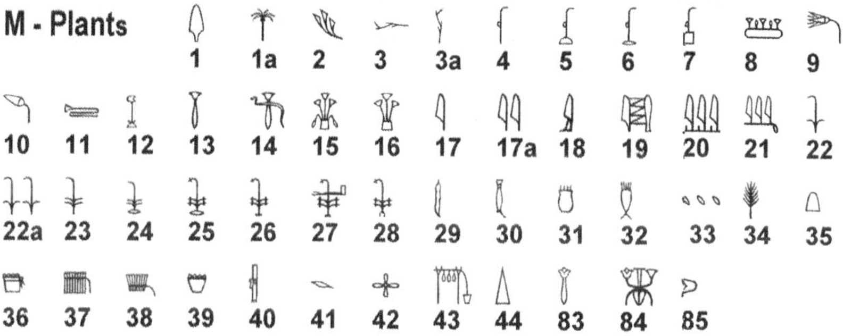

1 1a 2 3 3a 4 5 6 7 8 9
10 11 12 13 14 15 16 17 17a 18 19 20 21 22
22a 23 24 25 26 27 28 29 30 31 32 33 34 35
36 37 38 39 40 41 42 43 44 83 84 85

N - Sky, Earth, Water

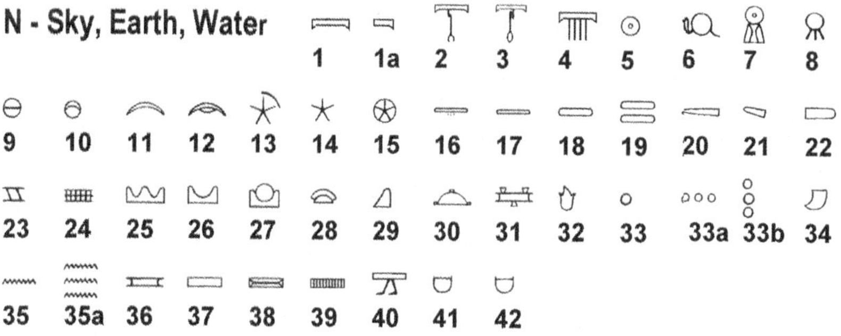

1 1a 2 3 4 5 6 7 8
9 10 11 12 13 14 15 16 17 18 19 20 21 22
23 24 25 26 27 28 29 30 31 32 33 33a 33b 34
35 35a 36 37 38 39 40 41 42

O - Buildings and Parts

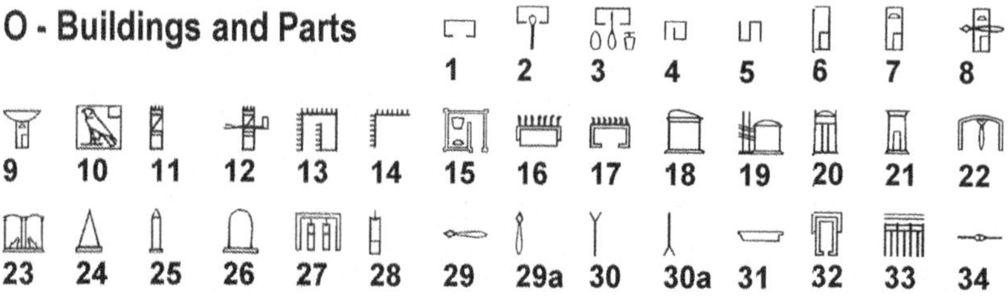

1 2 3 4 5 6 7 8
9 10 11 12 13 14 15 16 17 18 19 20 21 22
23 24 25 26 27 28 29 29a 30 30a 31 32 33 34

O - Buildings and Parts (cont)

35 36 36a 37 38 39 40

41 42 43 44 45 46 47 48 49 50 51

P - Ships and Parts

1 1a 2 3 4 5 6 7 8

8a 9 10 11

Q - Domestic Furniture

1 2 3 4 5 6 7

R - Temple Furniture

1 2 3 4 5 6 7 8 9

10 11 12 13 14 15 16 17 18 19 20 21 22 23

24 25

S - Crowns, Dress, Staves

1 2 3 4 5 6 7 8

9 10 11 12 12a 13 14 14a 15 16 17 18 19 20

21 22 17a 23 24 25 26 27 28 29 30 31 32 33

34 V39 35 36 37 38 39 40 41 42 43 44 45 81

81a 82

T - War, Hunting, Butchery

1 2 3 4 5 6 7 7a

8 8a 9 9a 10 10a Aa32 11 12 13 14 15 16 17

18 19 20 21 22 23 24 25 26 27 28 29 30 31

32 33 34 35 81 82

U - Agriculture, Crafts, etc

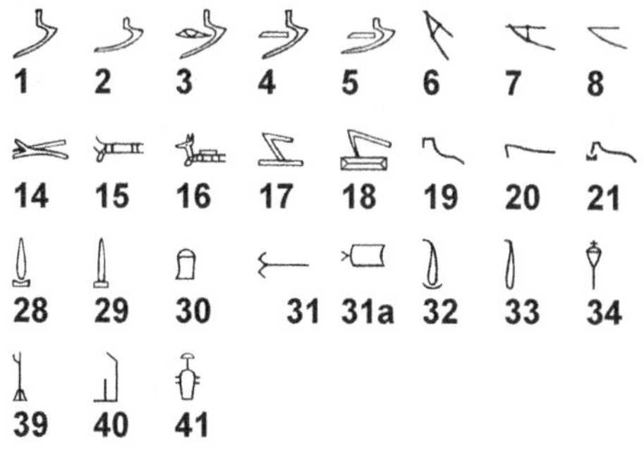

V - Rope, Fibre, Baskets, Bags, etc

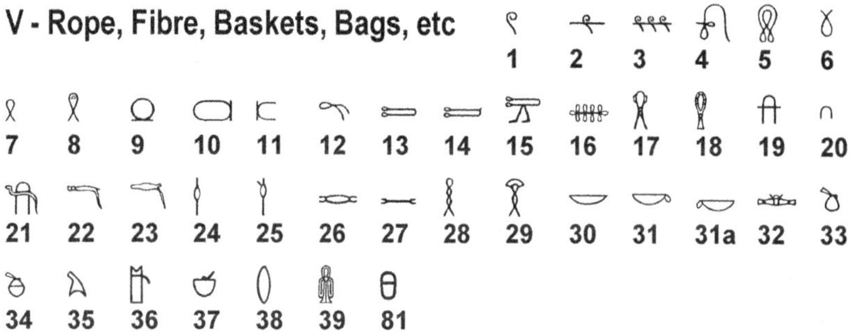

W - Vessels

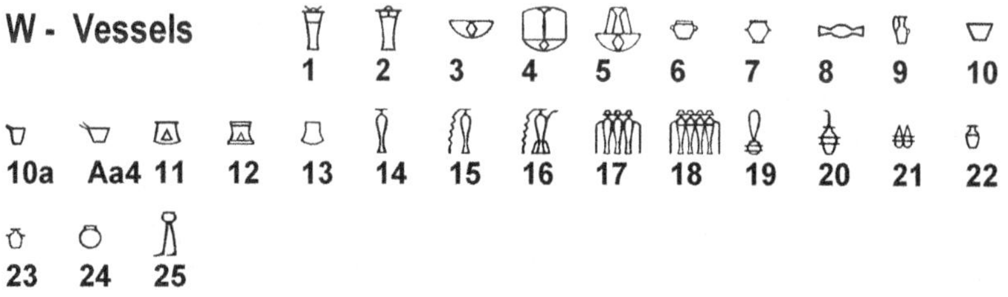

X - Loaves and Cakes

Y - Writing, Games, Music

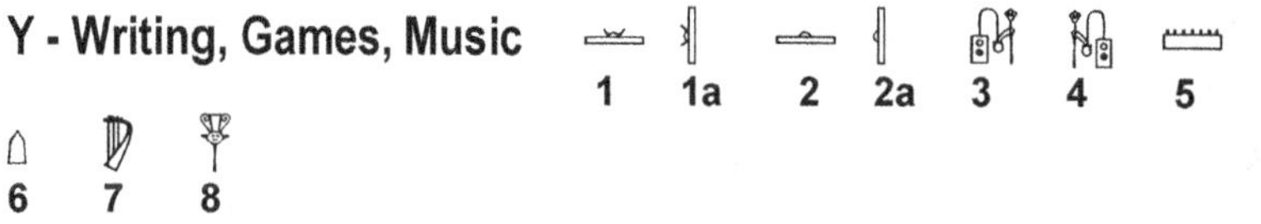

Z - Strokes, Signs, etc.

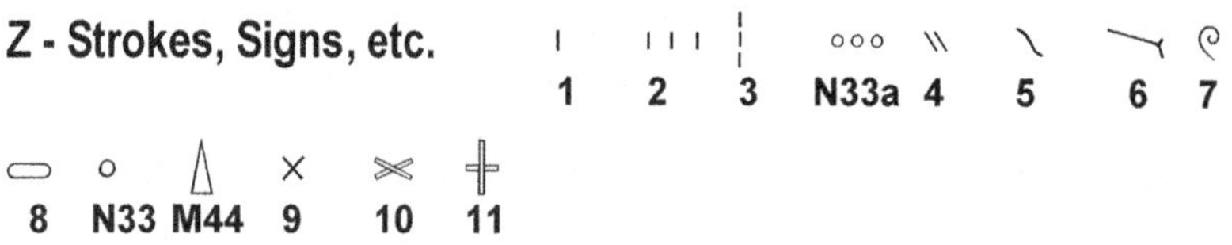

Aa - Unclassified

						1	2	3	4	5	6	7	7a	8
9	10	11	11a	12	12a	13	14	15	16	17	18	19	20
21	22	23	24	25	26	27	28	29	30	31	32	80	

By Shape - Low Broad Signs

N1	N37	N38	N39	S32	N18	S82	X4a	Z8	X4	X5
N16	N17	N20	O36a							
Aa10	Aa11	Aa12	Aa13	Aa14	Aa15	N35	Aa8	Aa9	V26	V27
R24	W8	V32	Y1	Y2	R4	N11	N12	F42	D24	D25
D13	D15	F20	Z6	F33	T2	T7	F30	V22	V23	R5
R6	O34	V2	V3	S24	R22	R23	T11	O29	T1	T21
U19	U20	U21	D17	U31	T9	T9a	T10	F32	V14	F46
F47	F48	F49	M11	U17	U18	U14	Aa7	Aa7a	F18	D51
U15	U16	Aa24	N31	O31	N36	D14	D21	D22	T30	T31
T33	D48	V30	V31	V31a	W3	S12	N30	O42	O43	V16

By Shape - Tall Thin Signs

M40 Aa28 Aa29 P11 D16 T34 T35 U28 U29 U32 U33 S43 U36

T8 T8a M13 M17 H6 H6a M4 M12 S29 M29 M30 S37 R14

R15 R16 R17 P6 S40 R19 S41 F10 F11 F12 S38 S39 T14

T15 T13 Aa26 O30 Aa21 U39 F45 O44 Aa27 R8 R9 T7a Aa32

T3 T4 V24 V25 U23 S42 U34 S36 F28 U26 U27 U24 R11

U25 Y8 F35 F36 U41 W19 P8 T22 T23 Z11 S44 Aa25 M44

V38 Aa30 Aa31 Aa20 V36 F31 M32 L7 V17 V18 S34 V39 Q7

T18 T19 T20 R21 O28 O11 O36 V28 V29 M3a M83 T10a T82

By Shape - Low Narrow Signs

Q3 O39 Z8 O47 N21 N22 N23 N29 X7 O45 O46 Y6 M35 Aa16

X1 X2 X3 N28 Aa17 I6 W10 W10a Aa4 R7 M39 M36 F43 F41

N34 U30 W11 W12 W13 T28 N41 N42 V37 M31 F34 W6 W7 W21

W20 V6 V33 V34 V7 V8 S20 V20 V19 Aa19 Aa2 Aa3 N32 F52

V35 H8 M41 F51 D11 K6 L6 F21 D26 N33 D12 S21 N5 N9

N10 Aa1 O48 O49 O50 X6 V9 S10 N6 N8 S11 N15 M42 F38

V1 Z7 Z9 Z10 M85 N1a X80 Aa80

The Essentials from Museum Tours Press

available from
museum-tours.com
Amazon.com and other retailers

Hieroglyphic Sign List: Based on the Work of Alan Gardiner - 5½" by 8½", soft cover, 132 pages, with about 800 Hieroglyphic signs, transliterations, meanings and examples. Also available in an easy-to-carry, 4¼" by 5½" spiral bound version. $12.95.

The Names of the Kings of Egypt: The Serekhs and Cartouches of Egypt's Pharaohs, along with Selected Queens - 5½" by 8½", soft cover, 122 pages, contains the Horus names, Prenomens and Nomens for 300 Kings and 29 Queens. Also available in a 4¼" by 5½" spiral bound version. $14.95.

Egyptian Glyphary: A Sign List Based Hieroglyphic Dictionary of Middle Egyptian - 5½" by 8½", soft cover, 294 pages, contains over 4,000 unique entries. A Glyphary™ is organized like a Sign List, with each sign followed by a list of words, and definitions, containing that sign. $14.95.

Hieroglyphic Dictionary: A Middle Egyptian Vocabulary - 5½" by 8½", soft cover, 188 pages, with over 4,000 unique entries, arranged alphabetically. It emphasizes words found in historical inscriptions. $14.95.

Urkunden Der 18. Dynastie - Facsimile edition of the 4 volume work by Kurt Sethe, out of print for over 100 years, is still one of the most highly referenced works in Egyptology. Each 6" by 9", soft cover volume contains over 300 pages. Soft cover with original German text and hand drawn hieroglyphs. $14.95 per volume.

Made in the USA
Coppell, TX
10 April 2021

53358156R10164